The End of th

THE END *of* THE BEGINNING

Lessons of the Soviet Collapse

Carlos Martinez

First published in January 2019

LeftWord Books
2254/2A Shadi Khampur
New Ranjit Nagar
New Delhi 110008
INDIA

LeftWord Books is the publishing division of
Naya Rasta Publishers Pvt. Ltd.

leftword.com

ISBN 978-93-80118-78-9

Printed and bound by Chaman Enterprises, Delhi

Contents

Introduction

Although a distance of more than a quarter-century separates us from that fateful day in December 1991 when the Union of Soviet Socialist Republics (USSR) ceased to exist, understanding of the Soviet collapse remains unsatisfactory and incomplete. The global working class is still reeling from the blows of that two-year period from 1989 to 1991 – when socialism was dismantled from Berlin to Khabarovsk. Yet, we still haven't fully understood the nature of those blows.

Such a situation must be remedied. Existing socialist states face many of the same external pressures that the Soviet Union faced; future socialist states will too. In addition to interference from the imperialist world, the socialist experiments thus far have faced a number of *internal* problems: how to maintain economic growth in the face of constantly changing needs and expectations; how to maintain revolutionary momentum through the second, third and fourth generations of the revolution; how to balance a revolutionary internationalist foreign policy with the need to maintain peaceful coexistence with the capitalist world; how to avoid economic and diplomatic isolation and to take advantage of the latest global developments in science and technology. These problems are faced by the remaining socialist countries, just as they were faced by the USSR.

In trying to locate solutions to such problems, the details of the Soviet collapse constitute some of the most important historical data we have available. The more our movement can learn about the Soviet experience, the better prepared we will be to prevent historic reverses and defeats in future, and the better equipped we will be to develop a compelling, convincing vision of socialism that is relevant in the here and now.

Needless to say, this book doesn't seek to present definitive answers. The disappearance of the USSR is a vastly complex subject, incorporating history, politics, economics, sociology, philosophy, military science, social psychology and more. Others know more and have done more thorough research than I have. The idea here is simply to present a historical outline, raise some questions, put forward some hypotheses, and contribute to the ongoing debate.

I make no apologies for taking a partisan perspective; of defending the achievements of the Soviet Union; of standing on the workers' side of the barricades in the global class war. If the reader is looking for a triumphalist, anti-communist account of the Soviet demise, such a thing can easily be found, but not here. The starting point of this book is that the immense problems faced by humanity cannot be solved within a political-economic framework of capitalism; that the transition towards socialism and communism is both desirable and necessary.

It is difficult to divide such a complex subject into neat segments, and the chapter headings I've ended up with are an unusual hybrid of chronological and thematic.

Chapter 1 highlights the positive aspects of the Soviet experience and seeks to break through the wall of McCarthyite propaganda that produces a popular imagining of the USSR as totalitarian, unjust and miserable.

Chapter 2 discusses the multitude of economic difficulties faced by the USSR in its last decades, and the various measures that were taken to address them.

Chapter 3 paints a picture of slow but steady ideological deterioration and decaying popular confidence from the 1950s onwards; a trickle that, by the late 1980s, had developed into an irreversible torrent of anti-communism and generalized dissatisfaction.

Chapter 4 outlines the ramping up of US-led imperialist destabilization and military pressure in the 1970s and '80s, with a particular focus on Ronald Reagan's 'full-court press', the arms race, and the war in Afghanistan.

Chapter 5 deals with the period from 1985 (when Mikhail Gorbachev became General Secretary of the Communist Party of the Soviet Union) to 1989, discussing the ideas of *perestroika* and *glasnost*, concepts that came to define the period of the collapse.

Chapter 6 moves on to the confusing and chaotic period of 1989–91, covering the rise of Yeltsin, the steady dismantling of Soviet power, the fall of socialist Europe, the attempts in August 1991 to save the USSR, and the details of how the world's first socialist state was torn apart.

Chapter 7 provides a brief overview of the effects of capitalist restoration on ordinary people in the former Soviet Union, as well as on the global working class.

The final chapter sums up the earlier material and offers some thoughts about the relevance of the Soviet experience to the remaining socialist countries.

CHAPTER 1

The Lion's Point of View

> Until the lions have their own historians, the history of the hunt will always glorify the hunter.
>
> – African proverb

Over a quarter of a century after the Soviet collapse and the end of the Cold War, the history of the USSR as told by mainstream historians is that it was a horrific, criminal enterprise; that Soviet socialism was the very antithesis of freedom and democracy; that the whole experiment was an unmitigated failure that has its clear antithesis in the success of Western free-market democracy. This is all received wisdom in Western Europe and North America, to such a degree that when anyone in the media spotlight questions it, they're treated like members of the Flat Earth Society.

These general, non-specific prejudices feed into what is surely the most prominent theme of modern politics, economics, history, philosophy and sociology: that communism is a wrongheaded and illogical ideology that contradicts the very essence of human nature.

Even within the political left, few are those that bother defending the record of the Soviet Union any more. We throw up our hands and say, 'We still believe in socialism, but the Russians got it wrong.' Perhaps *true socialism* has never been built; perhaps early 20th-century Russia, with its economic backwardness and vast peasant majority, wasn't a suitable environment for such an ambitious project; perhaps socialism was perverted and destroyed by the venality and ruthlessness of the Soviet leadership, in particular Joseph Stalin.

Whichever variant of the 'failure' narrative you choose, you're left with no special difficulty explaining why, on the 31st of December, 1991, the Union of Soviet Socialist Republics ceased to exist: it was a failed experiment, and failed experiments must eventually come to an end.

* * *

On December 21, 1982, Yuri Andropov, one of the key leaders of the USSR, offered his report on the 60th anniversary of the Revolution.

> The path traversed by the Soviet Union over the last sixty years is equivalent to a whole epoch. History perhaps has never known such a spectacular advance from a condition of backwardness, misery and ruin to the grandeur of a modern great power with highly advanced culture and steadily growing welfare of the people.

In reality, the task of understanding the Soviet implosion is not so simple. The Soviet Union has several world-historic achievements to its name. In the Soviet period, the peoples of the territories of the Soviet Union experienced an unprecedented improvement in living standards. Feudal property relations and backwardness were wiped out, and the Soviet Union emerged as a superpower – the second biggest economy in the world, at the cutting edge of several branches of science and technology. For the first time in Russian history, the curse of famine was overcome.

European fascism was defeated in large part through the efforts, sacrifices, heroism and creative brilliance of the Soviet people. Soviet people built and enjoyed the world's first comprehensive welfare state. Nobody that was willing and able to work went without work. Education and healthcare were comprehensive and free. Housing was often cramped, but universal and inexpensive. For the first time in history, the political and cultural supremacy of the working class was established: the government derived its credibility on the basis of how well it served the masses, not the wealthy. With the aid of the Soviet people, liberation movements around the world were able to break free from the shackles of colonialism and imperialism.

Mocking the histrionic anti-communism of mainstream historians, Michael Parenti writes in *Blackshirts and Reds*,

> To say that 'socialism doesn't work' is to overlook the fact that it did. In Eastern Europe, Russia, China, Mongolia, North Korea, and Cuba, revolutionary communism created a life for the mass of people that was far better than the wretched existence they had endured under feudal lords, military bosses, foreign colonizers, and Western capitalists. The end result was a dramatic improvement in living conditions for hundreds of millions of people on a scale never before or since witnessed in history.... State socialism transformed desperately poor countries into modernized societies in which everyone had enough food, clothing, and shelter; where elderly people had secure pensions; and where all children (and many adults) went to school and no one was denied medical attention.

Socialism in practice conclusively solved many of the worst of humanity's problems; problems which capitalism had not (and *still* has not) been able to resolve. Boris Ponomarev, a leading theoretician of the Communist Party of the Soviet Union, wrote,

> Socialism has ended for good the problem of unemployment which is the worst and most insurmountable social problem in the capitalist world. The countries of the socialist community have introduced blanket social security schemes covering the entire population, free medical care and education, guaranteed housing along with many other social blessings and economic rights enjoyed by one and all. Socialism has guaranteed

> equitable distribution of material and cultural benefits . . . Socialism has ended unequal pay for women and youth . . .

Inasmuch as many modern capitalist societies also established welfare systems, universal education and some level of gender equality, this is in no small part thanks to the path forged by the socialist countries. Bruni de la Motte and John Green note that 'the ruling establishments feared socialist revolutions in their own countries and realized that only by offering working people an amelioration of their conditions and granting increased rights in the workplace would they be able to head off more revolutionary demands'. Of course, workers fought for these rights, but their bargaining position was significantly boosted by the existence of a far-reaching system of rights and social insurance in the socialist world. It is no coincidence that, since the demise of European socialism, these rights have been subjected to ruthless attack.

* * *

In assessing the achievements of the Soviet Union, it's important to recognize the low base from which it started. Pre-revolutionary Russia was characterized by widespread hunger, stark authoritarianism, obscene inequality, pervasive racist and anti-Semitic scapegoating, and brutal exploitation. Workers and peasants were denied access to even basic education. The bankrupt tsarist regime (and indeed the provisional government after the February 1917 revolution) thought nothing of sacrificing the lives of millions of ordinary people in the name of colonial expansion.

The tendency in Western academia is to compare the lot of Soviet workers with that of middle-class North Americans in the 21st century. The conditions of tsarist Russia provide a much more meaningful frame of reference. As David M. Kotz and Fred Weir point out,

> In 1917 the Russian economy lagged far behind the dynamic capitalism of the great powers. In 1980, some sixty years after the Russian Revolution, the Soviet Union was one pole of a bipolar world. It had been transformed into an urban, industrialized country of 265 million people. By such measures as life expectancy, caloric intake, and literacy, the Soviet Union had reached the ranks of the developed countries. It gave economic and military aid to many countries around the world. It was a leader in many areas of science and technology. It launched the first space satellite. In some more prosaic fields, ranging from specialized metals, to machines for seamless welding of railroad tracks, to eye surgery equipment, it was a world leader. Its performing artists and athletes were among the world's best. With its Warsaw Pact allies, it was the military equal of the United States-led NATO alliance.

* * *

The Soviet Union was the first state to explicitly represent the demands of the working class and oppressed people. As Lenin put it in 1917, the significance of the revolution 'is, first of all, that we shall have a Soviet government, our own organ of power, in which the bourgeoisie will have no share whatsoever. The oppressed masses will themselves create a power. The old state apparatus will be shattered to its foundations and a new administrative apparatus set up in the form of the Soviet organizations.'

At the most basic level, the benefits of economic growth were directed towards ordinary people rather than a capitalist class. While GDP growth was respectable in the US, Western Europe and Japan in the post-war period, it had its clear counterpart in ever-widening inequality. The rich became much, much richer; conditions of life for the poor improved little. According to Albert Szymanski (1984),

'Over the entire 1940–1980 period the real wages of Soviet factory and office workers increased by a factor of 3.7 times. By way of comparison it should be noted that the real wages of all US workers declined by about 1% a year over the 1970s and early 1980s.' Furthermore, in the Soviet Union, basic foodstuffs, housing and transport were all heavily subsidized. Baseline costs – housing, transport, medicine – accounted for something like *15 per cent of family income*, as opposed to *50 per cent in the US*. Education at *all levels* – from nursery to post-graduate – was *free*.

The Soviet Union was incomparably more egalitarian than the capitalist countries. As Parenti put it, 'The income spread between highest and lowest earners in the Soviet Union was about five to one. In the United States, the spread in yearly income between the top multibillionaires and the working poor is more like 10,000 to 1.'

Ending unemployment was a momentous breakthrough. The individual's right to productive employment is recognized in the 1948 United Nations Universal Declaration of Human Rights, and yet it is near-impossible to guarantee such a right under capitalism, which mandates the existence of a pool of unemployed workers (Marx's 'reserve army of labour') to exert downward pressure on wages. Conversely, in a socialist system, where the fruits of labour are shared by the people rather than being monopolized by the capitalist class, the existence of unemployment is a shocking waste of resources. The Soviet Union was therefore the first modern industrial economy to eliminate long-term unemployment. The consequences of this in terms of people's well-being are huge; after all, unemployment is widely regarded as the number one socio-economic problem in the capitalist world.

Hewlett Johnson, wrote of the social impact of full employment and a welfare state in his classic study *The Socialist Sixth of the World* (1939), based on his numerous tours to the USSR in the 1930s:

> The vast moral achievements of the Soviet Union are in no small measure due to the removal of fear. Fear haunts workers in a capitalist land. Fear of dismissal, fear that a thousand workless men stand outside the gate eager to get his job, breaks the spirit of a man and breeds servility. Fear of unemployment, fear of slump, fear of trade depression, fear of sickness, fear of an impoverished old age lies with crushing weight on the mind of the worker. A few weeks' wages only lie between him and disaster. He lacks reserves.
>
> Nothing strikes the visitor to the Soviet Union more forcibly than the absence of fear. . . . No fear for maintenance at the birth of a child cripples the Soviet parents. No fear for doctors' fees, school fees, or university fees. No fear of under-work, no fear of over-work. No fear of wage reduction, in a land where none are unemployed. . . . So long as work is needed, work is free to all. Workers are in demand in the Soviet Union; and wages rise.

Russia's rich traditions of music, literature and theatre were combined with the abundant store of folk traditions from around the Soviet Union, producing a culture that was inclusive, accessible, innovative and proud. Most importantly, cultural life was not the preserve of the rich or the intellectuals but was the collective property of the masses. As Keeran and Kenny (2004) put it,

> UNESCO reported that Soviet citizens read more books and saw more films than any other people in the world. Every year the number of people visiting museums equalled nearly half the entire population, and attendance at theatres, concerts, and other performances surpassed the total population. The government made a concerted effort to raise the literacy and living standards of the most backward areas and to encourage the cultural expression of the more than a hundred nationality groups that constituted the Soviet Union. In Kirghizia [Kyrgyzstan], for example,

only one out of every five hundred people could read and write in 1917, but fifty years later nearly everyone could.

Throughout the socialist world, people had access to education and the opportunities that came with it. Furthermore, they were engaged in socially productive labour; their work contributed to the well-being of their community and their country – unlike so much work in capitalist society that contributes exclusively to the production of exchange values (profit) and so little to ordinary people's quality of life as well as contributes to waste (on weapons production, for instance).

* * *

Breaking with the brutal colonialism of the tsarist empire, the Soviet government succeeded in uniting dozens of nations and ethnicities into a multi-national state based on mutual respect and tolerance. 'Complete equality of rights for all nations', as Lenin put it, 'the right of nations to self-determination; the unity of the workers of all nations' was a highly advanced slogan *anywhere* in the early 20th century, but particularly so in Russia, that 'prison house of nations'.

The resolution of the national question in the Soviet Union was a historic achievement. At the root of the Soviet approach was Marx's famous teaching in a note to Bakunin in 1870, that '*any nation that oppresses another nation forges its own chains*'. Different nations, with their varying religions, ethnicities, histories and traditions, were brought together in a multi-national state that actively worked to overcome the Russian chauvinism and domination constructed over centuries under the tsars. Formerly proud nations such as Azerbaijan and Georgia – vibrant centres along the Silk Road that had suffered tyranny and enforced backwardness as part of the Russian empire – became equal players in a socialist union, in the process experiencing extraordinary improvements in living standards, education levels, access to cultural facilities, and so on. The Egyptian Marxist economist Samir Amin wrote:

> The Soviet system . . . gave these republics, regions, and autonomous districts, established over huge territories, the right to their cultural and linguistic expression, which had been despised by the tsarist government. The United States, Canada, and Australia never did this with their indigenous peoples and are certainly not ready to do so now. The Soviet government did much more: it established a system to transfer capital from the rich regions of the Union (western Russia, Ukraine, Belorussia, later the Baltic countries) to the developing regions of the east and south. It standardized the wage system and social rights throughout the entire territory of the Union, something the Western powers never did with their colonies, of course. In other words, the Soviets invented an authentic development assistance, which presents a stark contrast with the false development assistance of the so-called donor countries of today.

Once the radical movements in the Central Asian and Caucasian areas of the Russian empire had established Soviet power, the new regimes immediately got on with the job of undoing the legacy of Russian domination, engaging in radical land distribution and giving land that had been seized by Russian settlers to local peasants. This was combined, as Szymanski notes, with 'a wide range of economic, social and cultural improvements in people's lives, including mass literacy campaigns, universal education, modernization of agriculture, industrialization, and the provision of basic medical and welfare services'.

The eastern republics of the USSR experienced a period of unprecedented economic and cultural advancement, shared by the whole population. Before 1917, literacy in the oppressed Central Asian republics of the Russian empire ranged from four per cent to 16 per cent. After three decades of the USSR's existence, literacy was more or less universal throughout the union. Compare this with capitalist India, where even today the literacy rate is only 74 per cent – or perhaps more pertinently with Afghanistan (which shares a border and significant cultural heritage with Turkmenistan, Uzbekistan and Tajikistan), where the literacy rate today is among the lowest in the world at 31 per cent (17 per cent for women).

* * *

The Soviet people attempted to build a society free from racism. Just as 'you can't have capitalism without racism' (Malcolm X), the Soviet Union was built on the premise that you can't have socialism *with* racism. The constitution was unequivocal: 'Any direct or indirect restriction of the rights of, or, conversely, any establishment of direct or indirect privileges for, citizens on account of their race or nationality, as well as any advocacy of racial or national exclusiveness or hatred and contempt, is punishable by law.' The most palpable difference in these terms was the treatment of Jewish people before and after the revolution. During the tsarist period, Jews had been subjected to vicious, violent anti-Semitism, including officially-sanctioned pogroms. Russia had been a centre of the age-old European anti-Semitic scapegoating that gave rise to the horrors of Nazism. Szymanski notes, 'Jews were systematically excluded from privileged positions, and many were driven out of the country by discrimination and pogroms in the generation before the 1917 Revolution, large numbers of whom settled in the USA.'

After the revolution, expression of anti-Semitism was made a criminal offence. Indeed, 'Jewish intellectuals and workers were disproportionately active in the revolutionary movement in the Russian Empire. In 1922, Jews represented 5.2% of Communist Party membership (about five times their percentage of the population).'

Soviet newspapers also gave a great deal of attention to the plight of Black people in the US. Many prominent African-Americans visited the Soviet Union and were moved to comment on how much better they were treated there than in the country of their birth. The legendary African-American civil rights activist and Pan-African, W.E.B. Du Bois, wrote that

> The Soviet Union seems to me the only European country where people are not more or less taught and encouraged to despise and look down on some class, group or race. I know countries where race and colour prejudice show only slight manifestations, but no white country where race and colour prejudice seems so absolutely absent. In Paris I attract some attention; in London I meet elaborate blankness; anywhere in America I get anything from complete ignoring to curiosity, and often insult. In Moscow, I pass unheeded. Russians quite naturally ask me information; women sit beside me quite confidently and unconsciously. Children are uniformly courteous. (Cited in Mandel 1985)

* * *

> In the course of two years, Soviet power in one of the most backward countries of Europe did more to emancipate women and to make their status equal to that of the 'strong' sex than all the advanced, enlightened, 'democratic' republics of the world did in the course of 130 years.
>
> – Lenin, 1919

The Soviet Union was for many decades the world leader in developing women's rights. Article 122 of the 1936 constitution established not only the principle of gender equality but the means by which the state would facilitate it:

> Women in the USSR are accorded equal rights with men in all spheres

> of economic, state, cultural, social and political life. The possibility of exercising these rights is ensured to women by granting them an equal right with men to work, payment for work, rest and leisure, social insurance and education, and by state protection of the interests of mother and child, pre-maternity and maternity leave with full pay, and the provision of a wide network of maternity homes, nurseries and kindergartens.

Family law was written so as to create a context for a flourishing of women's rights. Subsidized childcare was made universal, with the result that, by the late 1970s, the percentage of women in work was 83 per cent (compared with 55 per cent in the US), and over 40 per cent of professional scientists were female. According to Szymanski, in 1970, there were *more women physicians in the USSR than throughout the rest of the world*, with *about 20 times more than in the US*. He concludes that 'women are considerably more independent of men, and far greater opportunities are open to them than ever before, or that exist for women in comparable capitalist countries'. These are remarkable achievements, particularly in view of the patriarchal backwardness of the Russian empire under the tsars.

* * *

In comparing the progress made in the Soviet Union between 1917 and 1991 with the progress made in the capitalist world in the same period, it is crucial to bear in mind that capitalist progress was built on a bedrock of colonialism and imperialism. Industrialization and modernization in Britain would not have taken place without the grand-scale theft of productive land in the Americas, the transatlantic slave trade, and the colonial subjugation of India, Ireland and much of Africa. US-led economic progress in the 20th century rested on the profits of neo-colonial exploitation of the larger part of the globe. Not only was Soviet progress more impressive in absolute terms, but it was many times more impressive for having been achieved without recourse to imperialism. Yegor Ligachev observes,

> It should be kept in mind that everything we achieved was the result of our own efforts, whereas the developed capitalist countries accumulated much of their wealth by the open plunder of colonial peoples in the past and by ferrying cheap natural resources out of Third World countries today, exploiting their cheap workforce. In this way the capitalist countries have secured a relatively high standard of living for their populations.

More than the Soviet Union not engaging in imperialist exploitation, it engaged in the *opposite* of imperialist exploitation, seeing itself as a key engine of the global anti-colonial and anti-imperialist movement; an all-weather friend to the oppressed and struggling peoples of Asia, Africa and Latin America. This position was not taken purely out of goodwill and socialist morality but also as a means of developing the broadest possible unity against imperialism. In Lenin's words, '[The European working class] will not be victorious without the aid of the working people of all the oppressed colonial nations, first and foremost, of Eastern nations.'

The Soviet Union made significant sacrifices in order to support anti-colonial liberation movements (including the ANC in South Africa, the MPLA in Angola, PAIGC in Guinea-Bissau, Frelimo in Mozambique) and progressive states (including the people's democracies of central and eastern Europe, Cuba, Vietnam, Korea, Mongolia, Afghanistan, Angola, Mozambique, Mali, Guinea, Ghana, Ethiopia, India, Egypt, Libya, Grenada, Nicaragua, Indonesia, and more). This support was not simply tokenistic; indeed, in many cases – including the historic victory of the Vietnamese patriotic forces – it was decisive. Fidel Castro went so far as to say in a memorable speech at Red Square (Moscow) in 1963,

> Without the existence of the Soviet Union, Cuba's socialist revolution would have been impossible. . . . This means that without the existence of the Soviet Union, the imperialists would have strangled any national-liberation revolution in Latin America. . . . Had the Soviet Union not existed, the imperialists would not even have had to resort to weapons. They would have strangled such a revolution with hunger. They would have liquidated it by only an economic blockade. But because the Soviet Union exists, it proved impossible to liquidate our revolution.

The Soviet Union served as a key support base for the other projects of socialist transformation in the 20th century, including the Chinese Revolution, which over the course of the last eight decades has comprehensively rejuvenated the Chinese nation, putting an end to feudal backwardness and colonial domination and making China a great world power. As Mao Zedong himself said, soon after the victory of the revolution, 'If the Soviet Union did not exist, if there were no victory of the Anti-Fascist Second World War and no defeat of Japanese imperialism, . . . if there were no sum-total of these things, could we have won victory? Obviously not. It would also be impossible to consolidate the victory when it was won.'

Paul Robeson remembered the USSR's principled support for Ethiopia against Mussolini's Italy, and for the native population of South Africa against the white supremacist government, concluding that '*the Soviet Union is the friend of the African and the West Indian peoples*' (Foner 1998).

* * *

After the Paris Commune of 1871, which lasted only two months, the October Revolution was the world's first attempt to build a socialist society, to put an end to the brutality, inequality and inefficiency of capitalism. As such, Boris Ponomarev wrote, October 'dispelled the myth of capitalism's immutability as a "natural order of things". It demonstrated that capitalism was not eternal and its replacement by socialism was on the agenda of history.'

In its 74-year existence, the Soviet Union succeeded in creating a completely different type of society: one that deeply valued equality, shared prosperity, social justice, solidarity, culture and education. It made greater economic, social, scientific and cultural progress than its competitors in the capitalist world during the period of its existence. And this was done in spite of the extraordinary human and economic losses it sustained defending itself against foreign aggression (in the 'civil war' of 1918–21 and the German invasion/occupation of the Soviet Union, 1941–44). Gennady Zyuganov, veteran Russian communist and current leader of the Communist Party of the Russian Federation, notes with justifiable pride:

> The socialism that was built in the USSR and a number of other countries was, of course, far from perfect. But it exhibited some historic achievements. The socialist system enabled us to create a powerful state with a developed national economy. We were the first to venture into the cosmos. Our culture reached unprecedented heights. We were justly proud of our achievements in science, theatre, film, education, music, ballet, literature, and the visual arts. Much was done to develop physical culture, sports, and folk arts. Every citizen of the USSR had the right to work, free education and medical care, and a secure childhood and old age. Appropriate budgetary allocations subsidized housing and provided for the needs of children. People were sure of their tomorrow. A workable alternative to capitalism was created in our own country and in other socialist countries. . . . And these changes were made in the shortest period recorded in world history for such a transformation. (Zyuganov 1997)

Like any country, the Soviet Union suffered its fair share of complex problems and was guilty of its fair share of mistakes, but by no reasonable measure can the Soviet period be deemed a failure. The 'failed experiment' hypothesis of the Soviet collapse is merely an extension of old-fashioned Cold War propaganda.

CHAPTER 2

Socialism in the Queue

> We do not forget for a moment that we have committed and are committing numerous mistakes and are suffering numerous reverses. How can reverses and mistakes be avoided in a matter so new in the history of the world as the building of an unprecedented type of state edifice! We shall work steadfastly to set our reverses and mistakes right and to improve our practical application of Soviet principles, which is still very, very far from being perfect.
>
> – Lenin, 1921

The USSR achieved a great deal in its brief existence, but there were nonetheless problems within the Soviet Union that require our attention. Building the first socialist state in a world still dominated by aggressive, expansionist capitalism was a near-impossible task, analogous to a small child learning to walk while people stand nearby trying to push her over.

* * *

Analysis of the available data indicates that, up until around 1975, the Soviet economy was working very well. Even Henry Kissinger was moved to declare in 1960 that, 'starting from a position of substantial inferiority in almost all areas, the Soviet Union has caught up with and surpassed us in more categories than are comforting' (quoted in Westad 2005).

British economics professor Philip Hanson – by no means an ideological supporter of the Soviet Union – writes,

> Well into the 1970s the Soviet Union was seldom described as failing. Its economy tended, up to the early 1970s, to grow faster than that of the United States. For a generation or more after the Second World War, the traditional Soviet aim of 'catching up and overtaking' the West was not patent nonsense. . . . In the course of thirty years, from the end of the Second World War, the Soviet Union had recovered from wartime devastation and massive loss of life. It had made remarkable strides in military technology. It had broken the US monopolies of, successively, the atomic bomb, the hydrogen bomb and inter-continental ballistic missiles. . . . And the lives of Soviet citizens had at the same time improved immensely.

This was also, of course, a period of growth for the major capitalist economies, but the Soviet growth rate was much higher than the rate in the capitalist bloc. Throughout the post-war period up until the mid-1970s, Soviet industrial growth was three times that of the US. In fact, Michael Roberts (2017) points out, 'from 1928 to 1970, the USSR was the fastest growing economy except for Japan'. What's more, the Soviet economy was not susceptible to the cycle of booms and busts that plagues capitalist economies.

Economic success was not manifested purely in terms of growth figures or scientific achievement; it was reflected in a steadily improving quality of life for ordinary people. After a period of extraordinary upheaval – the First World War, the Revolution, the war of intervention, rapid industrialization and agricultural collectivization, and then the Second World War (in which the Soviet Union lost an estimated 27 million people) – the period from the mid-1940s to the mid-1970s was one of steady rebuilding, in a relatively peaceful external environment.

For example, as Kotz and Weir (1997) find, 'In 1960 about one out of two Soviet families owned a radio, one out of ten a television, and one out of twenty-five a refrigerator. By 1985 there was an average of one of each per family.' Everybody had work – a vastly important quality-of-life indicator – and the quality of state-provided services such as education and healthcare continued to improve.

* * *

These successes were not built on the base of any deep-rooted strength in the pre-revolutionary Russian economy. Russia before October 1917 was, as Irfan Habib (2017) notes, 'In terms of every economic index among the most backward and poorest of European countries. Its per capita income in 1913 was about 102 roubles, compared to that of England, 463 roubles, France, 355, and Germany, 292.' The industrial working class constituted just two per cent of the population. Following the First World War and the war of intervention, the economy was utterly decimated.

In a resolution discussing the then-recent collapse of the USSR, the 14th Congress of the Communist Party of India (Marxist) described the extraordinary obstacles over which the Soviet people had to climb in order to modernize:

> The relatively low level of productive forces and the associated backward production and social relations had to be substantially raised, and at a breakneck speed, bypassing the stage of capitalism, to levels that could sustain socialist construction. This had to be done relying purely on internal resources, without access to the higher techniques of production developed by capitalism and in an hostile international atmosphere when world capitalism tried all methods at its disposal to asphyxiate socialism. It is in fact a testimony to the superiority of the socialist system that such a gigantic task could be achieved.

What drove Soviet economic success, allowing it to emerge from the chaos of war, quickly industrialize, develop to the level of being able to defeat the Nazi war machine, and establish a standard of living comparable to middle-income European countries was, first and foremost, the system of central planning set in motion in 1928 with the first five-year plan. Although this assertion flies in the face of established economic wisdom that 'planned economies don't work', the extent and rate of development during the five-year plans is indisputable.

Kotz and Weir explain that the system of central planning

> achieved a very high rate of investment, which made possible the rapid creation of a whole set of new industries. It was able to rapidly educate and train the population for industrial work and rapidly shift the population into better-paying, more productive urban industrial jobs. . . . The highly centralized planning system also proved effective at the process of building at least the first stages of a modern urban society, with a reasonably high level of amenities and consumer goods for the population. . . . Soviet central planning proved able to rapidly build urban infrastructure (transportation, communication, power, etc.), construct new housing, and manufacture new consumer goods.

The Soviet economic system was particularly well suited to the tasks of rapid industrialization and preparation for war. A predominantly rural, technologically backward, poorly educated country was transformed into a modern industrial economy with a high level of education; a world power capable of defeating the Nazi war machine. Almost exactly ten years before the Nazis launched their attack on the Soviet Union, Stalin famously summed up the essential challenge of the era: 'We are fifty or a hundred years behind the advanced countries. We must make good this distance in ten years. Either we do it, or they crush us.' The first and second five-year plans enabled the Soviet people to rise to that challenge. It is unlikely that any other economic framework would have allowed such rapid development; no capitalist economic programme has brought about large-scale modernization in so short a period of time. Economist Ha-Joon Chang writes of this achievement,

> To everyone's surprise, the early Soviet industrialization was a big success, most graphically proven by its ability to repel the Nazi advance on the Eastern Front during the Second World War. Income per capita is estimated to have grown at 5 per cent per year between 1928 and 1938 – an astonishingly rapid rate in a world in which income typically grew at 1–2 per cent per year.

* * *

Soviet economic performance remained strong through the 1950s and 1960s: the post-war construction was another heroic effort and a victory for socialism. Living standards increased rapidly, and the growth rate remained higher than that of the United States. However, this trend did not continue. 'From 20 per cent the size of the US economy in 1944', writes Jude Woodward (2017), the Soviet economy peaked at '44 per cent that of the US by 1970 ($1,352 billion to $3,082 billion) but had fallen back to 36 per cent of the US by 1989 ($2,037 billion to $5,704 billion).'

In an essay written just after the USSR collapsed, Sitaram Yechury, General Secretary of the Communist Party of India (Marxist), wrote,

> By the mid-1970s, the Soviet economy showed declining trends in growth rates. This is for the first time since the introduction of the five-year plan that such a trend becomes visible. During the decade 1976 to 1985 the growth rates of both the national product and industrial production

declined. The plan targets were not achieved under the five-year plan of 1976–80 and 1981–85.

At a time when the geopolitical environment was starting to look relatively stable and promising – with the victory of the popular forces in Vietnam, Angola, Mozambique, Guinea-Bissau, Ethiopia, Zimbabwe, Laos, Cambodia, Ghana, Nicaragua and Afghanistan, and with the apparent possibility of a lasting *detente* between the US and USSR – internal economic problems arose in the Soviet Union that started to develop a creeping intractability. The reasons for this are manifold and disputed, but they centre round a failure of the existing economic system to produce significant gains in productivity from the mid-1960s onwards.

* * *

One great advantage the Soviet Union had in its socialist industrialization was the availability of huge quantities of fossil fuel. This continued to play an important role in Soviet economic growth, and furthermore helped to make up for weaknesses in other areas: difficult climate and soil conditions meant that food production had always been a challenge, and the changing needs and expectations of the post-war population made this problem ever more prominent. However, exports of primary goods generated sufficient hard currency to import food to supplement domestic produce.

By the 1970s, resource extraction was getting harder and more expensive. Existing oil fields became less productive, and new ones had to be found. Hanson (2014) writes,

> The depletion of oil, gas, coal and mineral resources in the European part of the USSR was forcing new natural-resource extraction to move

> east of the Urals – mainly to West Siberia. Extraction costs per unit of output were not necessarily higher in these new locations (though in some of them, in the far north, they were). However, these new regional developments required investment in transport, communications, housing and other infrastructure and the transport westwards of most of the energy and materials extracted, since the great bulk of manufacturing and urban settlement remained west of the Urals.

On top of this, the supply infrastructure was starting to suffer from inadequate investment. Kotz and Weir point out that 'by the mid-1970s the Soviet rail system had reached the limit set by its rail miles, and congestion began to slow deliveries. The failure to make timely investments in expanded rail miles and new sidings had created a serious bottleneck for the Soviet economy.'

Another important factor here is the tragic human loss from the war; horrific in its own right, it also had a knock-on effect on the post-war economy. Sam Marcy writes,

> Instead of having millions of excess worker-veterans returning, a whole layer of society, 20 million workers and peasants, had been torn away. A mighty economic force had thus been wiped out. These included men and women, both skilled and unskilled. Those who were killed were generally younger, which left an older population to tend to industry and agriculture. The USSR was deprived of a tremendous source of labour power, most particularly among the young on whom future generations generally rely. This set the USSR far behind the US, which had suffered no destruction at home and had lost 400,000 troops, or about one-fiftieth of the Soviet war dead. As soon as the war ended, the US was able to begin the production of consumer goods. These had been scarce during the war, but not nearly as scarce as in the USSR, which suffered the full-scale invasion of the Nazi armies.

* * *

> To win the victory in economic competition with capitalism it is necessary to surpass the advanced capitalist countries in the level of productivity of labour.
>
> – *Textbook on Political Economy*, Economics Institute of the USSR Academy of Sciences, 1954

A large portion of the early success of the planned economy was based on mobilizing vast human and material resources for a single project. Actual labour *productivity* – the level of output per unit of human labour – remained low compared to the advanced capitalist economies. Growth had relied on 'extensive' rather than 'intensive' production, with far less input from new technology or capital investment (compared with the US). Jonathan Aurthur explains in his 1977 book *Socialism in the Soviet Union* that

> At the beginning of the period of real industrialization (1927) the industrial proletariat was very small and its skilled sector even smaller. Eleven million peasants with virtually no technical or any other kind of training became industrial workers during the period of the First Five Year Plan. Under these conditions heavy industry could be built only by relying on large expenditures of human labour in the construction of big, basic, non-specialized factories set up to produce tractors one day and tanks the next day or the day after.

The backward state of transport infrastructure in the early days of industrialization led to the building of universal production centres. As Aurthur notes, the USSR built 'huge industrial complexes in which different kinds of production were centralized in one place near sources of minerals or other necessary raw materials'. These were a pragmatic way of surmounting the particular problems the USSR faced in its rapid industrial development in the 1920s and '30s, but they became a productivity bottleneck. 'It is a law of technology that the more types of jobs a tool can do, the less specialized and productive it will be', Aurthur wrote. Over-centralization of production ended up impeding the development of more modern, highly technical and capital-intensive industry.

By the 1970s, it was clear to the Soviet leadership that there was a problem. A qualitative leap in labour productivity was necessary if the USSR was to meet popular expectations. Yuri Andropov, a Politburo member and General Secretary of the CPSU from 1982 until his untimely death in early 1984, wrote in 1970, 'We have reached a stage where the factors of extensive economic growth have largely been exhausted, so that high rates of economic development and, consequently, of raising the material well-being of the Soviet people can be maintained mostly by intensifying social production.'

There are some obvious methods of increasing productive output per unit of labour employed: one is to get workers to work harder and more effectively; one is to reorganize the system of production so as to make it more efficient; one is to invest heavily in infrastructure related to production; another (typically the most important) is to leverage technology so that more work is done by machines and less by humans. The Soviet leadership tried all these methods and ultimately found them all extremely difficult. Rather than bringing about the steady increase in labour productivity that was so desperately needed, what actually happened was that, between 1975 and 1991, industrial labour productivity fell by as much as 50 per cent.

* * *

The central planning system implemented from 1928 was hugely successful; however, an economic framework that was appropriate in 1928 was not necessarily appropriate a quarter of a century later, in significantly changed circumstances. Indeed, in the post-war period, central planning came up against several stubborn problems.

Compared to the late 1920s, the Soviet economy of the 1950s was infinitely more complex and therefore more difficult to tightly plan. In the aftermath of the devastation of war and a widespread feeling that the Soviet people had earned an easier life in a context of 'peaceful coexistence', there was some re-focussing towards the production of consumer goods, meaning a far greater range of items to produce. A linear increase in the number of goods to produce meant an exponential increase in the complexity of the plan, which became increasingly fragile. Keeran and Kenny (2004), strong supporters of the planned economy, accept that 'planning became more difficult as the economy became larger and more complex. By 1953, the number of industrial enterprises reached 200,000 and the number of planning targets reached 5,000, up from 300 in the early 1930s and 2,500 in 1940.'

Michael Parenti outlines the issues in his book *Blackshirts and Reds*,

> Central planning was useful and even necessary in the earlier period of siege socialism to produce steel, wheat and tanks in order to build an industrial base and withstand the Nazi onslaught. But it eventually hindered technological development and growth, and proved incapable of supplying a wide-enough range of consumer goods and services. No computerized system could be devised to accurately model a vast and intricate economy.
>
> No system could gather and process the immense range of detailed information needed to make correct decisions about millions of production tasks. Top-down planning stifled initiative throughout the system. Stagnation was evident in the failure of the Soviet industrial establishment to apply the innovations of the scientific-technological revolution of the 1970s and 1980s, including the use of computer technology. Though the Soviets produced many of the world's best

mathematicians, physicists, and other scientists, little of their work found actual application.

One important problem highlighted by Parenti is that, with the prevailing system of planning based on ambitious numeric quotas, enterprise managers had very little incentive to introduce new technologies. 'They maintained their positions regardless of whether innovative technology was developed, as was true of their superiors and central planners.' Furthermore, the plan tended to encourage a mindset of quantity over quality. 'Under pressure to get quantitative results, managers often cut corners on quality. . . . For instance, since state buyers of meat paid attention to quantity rather than quality, collective farmers maximized profits by producing fattier animals. Consumers might not care to eat fatty meat but that was their problem. Only a foolish or saintly farmer would work harder to produce better quality meat for the privilege of getting paid less.'

* * *

One of the factors behind decreasing productivity was poor labour discipline; put simply, a lot of people were not working very hard.

Maintaining labour discipline in an economy with guaranteed full employment is challenging. Work – particularly tough, physical work – has to be incentivized in some way. Under capitalism, work is incentivized through fear of starvation: if you do not do a decent job, you can easily be replaced from among the 'reserve army of labour'. This is a cornerstone of capitalist economics. In fact, the advances in productivity in the capitalist countries in recent decades have been in no small part based on 'rationalization': replacing workers with robots, leaving low-wage, low-skill jobs for which there is ever-increasing competition in a global labour marketplace.

The Soviet Union never had a problem with unemployment; on the contrary it suffered from *overemployment* – there were more jobs to do than there were people to do them. Consequently, it rarely made sense for managers to sack people (and furthermore the system of labour rights made it very difficult to do so). But if people know they are very unlikely to be sacked, it makes it easy for them to game the system if they are inclined to do so. It was, in Parenti's words, a seller's market.

The issue of overemployment was more pronounced in the aftermath of the war, for the obvious reason that so many workers had been martyred, at a time when reconstruction of the country – and taking care of the sick and injured – demanded huge amounts of work.

Going by the experience of building socialism, it appears that in the early period of a revolution, it is more feasible to mobilize large numbers of people to work well on the basis of moral incentives; on the basis of common sacrifice for a better future. Not to mention that the initial phase of a revolution is profoundly empowering: it unleashes the creative energy of the masses, which feeds into more and better production. But clearly it is difficult to maintain this momentum over the course of multiple generations. Raúl Castro brought this issue to life in his description (just two decades into the Cuban Revolution) of the spread and effect of labour discipline problems in Cuba:

> The lack of work discipline, unjustified absences from work, deliberate go-slows so as not to surpass the norms – which are already low and poorly applied in practice – so that they won't be changed . . . In contrast to capitalism, when people in the countryside worked an exhausting 12-hour workday and more, there are a good many instances today especially in agriculture, of people working no more than four or six hours. . . . We know that in many cases heads of brigades and foremen make a deal with workers to meet the norm in half a day and then go off and work for the other half for some nearby small private farmer for extra income . . . or

> do two or three norms in a day and report them over other days on which they don't go to work. . . . All these 'tricks of the trade' in agriculture are also to be found in industry, transportation service, repair shops and many other places where there's rampant buddyism, cases of 'you do me a favour and I'll do you one' and pilfering on the side. (Quoted in Parenti 2001)

In the post-war period in the USSR, there was an emerging popular sentiment that, having sacrificed so much and having established a new level of geostrategic security through the emergence of friendly socialist governments in seven of twelve bordering countries, life should get easier and society should move towards fulfilling the socialist promise of common prosperity. For the leading capitalist powers, an easier life was established through exploitation of the poorer sections of the working class and through neo-colonialism. For the Soviet Union, however, these options were not available. The way to have more food, better housing, better clothes, cars and so on was to produce more, to work more effectively.

The government of the time was keenly aware of the need to improve people's immediate quality of life. Hanson writes that Nikita Khrushchev, in power from 1956 to 1964, 'presided over a major switch of resources towards agriculture, improved incentives for food production, the launch of a badly needed housing programme, a shortening of the work week, a large cut in the armed forces and an easing of the priority for heavy industry'. However, 'what all these improvements were not accompanied by was any serious reform of the economic system'. Hanson concludes that 'the humane softening of the system that occurred under Khrushchev's rule probably contributed to the later slowdown'.

In addition to a reduced work week, the Khrushchev administration moved to reduce income inequality. Albert Szymanski (1979) observed that, between the mid-1950s and 1970s, the Soviets 'eliminated about half of the inequality in their income distribution (reducing the ratio of the highest decile's to the lowest decile's average wages from 8.1 to 4.1) – a radical reduction in inequality in a very short time'. During the same period in the United States, there was practically no change in income distribution. Although greater economic equality seems more consistent with socialist ideals, the reduction of wage disparities also may have impacted people's willingness to work and study.

* * *

From the beginning, the Soviet government emphasized the importance of technical innovation as a means of modernizing quickly and providing for people's needs. Indeed, a major part of the promise of socialism – particularly for relatively undeveloped countries – is that it constitutes a more advanced, more efficient path to development, freeing science and technology from the constraints imposed by profit, competition, endless intermediaries, exploitation and cyclical crises, and orienting them towards meeting people's needs.

In just a few decades, Soviet science was able to bridge the gap between the scientific backwardness of the old Russian empire and the heights of global progress. Great sacrifices were made in order to ensure scientific research received the level of investment it needed. A well-known Russian scientist, Boris Raushenbakh, complaining about the decline in research funding in post-Soviet Russia, remarked,

> In 1918–19, Lenin organized a whole series of scientific institutes, including the Central Institute for Aviation and Hydrodynamics, the Leningrad Institute of Physics and Technology (which produced world-famous scholars Kurchatov, Kapitsa, and Semenov), and the Academy of Agriculture. These huge institutions were created at a time when . . . the entire country was consumed by the flames of civil war.
>
> Under Stalin, a great number of institutes were created. In the

> mid-1930s, an independent Rockefeller commission, which had organized a philanthropic fund to finance science in poorly developed countries, visited our country. The commission's report was published. Its conclusion: science was better financed here than in western Europe. (Quoted in Ligachev 1996)

In many key areas of science and technology, the USSR was able to catch up with the West, even becoming a global leader in certain fields. However, by the mid-1970s, the leading capitalist countries were forging ahead of their socialist counterparts. Computers and robotics, which were starting to penetrate all areas of the Western capitalist economy, led to significant gains in productivity. Computerization dramatically increased the spread of information, and it fed into new developments in maths and other branches of knowledge. The Soviet Union, as Kotz and Weir found, 'largely failed to absorb the revolution in communication and information-processing brought by electronics and computers'. By the time of the Soviet collapse, use of computing in industry and military technology is reckoned to have been around twenty years behind that of the United States.

It is not immediately obvious why the Soviet Union would have lagged behind in the information revolution. Its education system was excellent, particularly in mathematics and science; it invested heavily in research; scientists were among the most respected (and best-paid) members of society; it was anxious to keep up with technological developments in the United States; and its planning system could have benefited enormously from the improvements in statistics, logistics and information distribution offered by computerization. While the working class in the capitalist countries has had a complicated relationship with computer technology (which, while improving life in many respects, has also contributed to unemployment and labour deregulation), the Soviet working class could have leveraged it to its full potential.

Soviet government and academic circles certainly showed an early interest in computing and cybernetics, and considerable research took place in this area. However, for a multitude of reasons, the gap between research and ground-level implementation was never bridged in the way it was in the United States. At ground level, with a heavy emphasis on annual production targets, there was minimal incentive for risk-averse enterprise managers to introduce sweeping technological changes, and in the absence of a centrally-mandated and society-wide information revolution, computerization was somewhat marginalized. This was recognized by some of the more economically-literate leaders, for example Andropov, who wrote,

> To introduce a new process or new technology, production should be reorganized one way or the other, and this affects the fulfilment of the plan. Moreover, one will be held responsible for failure to fulfil the plan, while all one will get for inadequate application of new technology will be just reproach. . . . It is necessary to see to it that those who boldly introduce new technology will not find themselves at a disadvantage.

No suitable means were found to resolve this problem.

Where enterprise managers *were* keen to innovate, they often faced stumbling blocks. Longstanding leader of the Communist Party of the Russian Federation, Gennady Zyuganov (1997), writes,

> Without access to financial resources, industrial enterprises could not update their equipment, introduce new technologies, or take advantage of the most recent achievements in science and engineering. The scientific establishment itself, except for the defence branches, lost the stimulus for development that should have been provided by demand for new projects and technical innovations.

Apart from the direct economic advantages it provided, the

spread of computing proved to be a powerful advertisement for Western capitalism. The United States could point (not entirely without justification) to the interaction between hobbyists, scientists, universities, start-up businesses and government departments as having provided an optimum environment for computing to flourish. Once computing hit the mainstream with the rise of mass-market PCs in the late 1970s and early 1980s, a virtuous cycle was created whereby the 'tinkering' of millions of people fed into rapid innovation and the further spread of the technology. It would have been difficult to replicate this pattern in the heavily centralized economic framework then prevailing in the USSR.

Once they realized they were falling behind, Soviet leaders hoped to catch up quickly through technology transfer – importing Western computers and reverse-engineering them. However, US policymakers deliberately made that difficult by imposing tight trade embargoes. In US ruling circles, the tension between wanting to profitably trade with the Soviet Union and wanting to punish it and prevent its growth is one of the defining foreign policy debates of the 1970s and '80s. The 'hawks' – those who favoured the punishment approach – won the argument more often than not. Their position was summed up by US President Ronald Reagan's secretary of defence, Frank Carlucci, in 1988: 'If the end result is that the Soviet Union modernizes its industrial and technological base and if some time in the 1990s it ends up as a society that can produce enormous quantities of weapons even more effectively than it does today, then we will have made an enormous miscalculation' (quoted in Marcy 1990).

Of course, US capitalism still struggles with this issue today in relation to China; it is in fact the basis of the US–China trade war initiated by the Trump presidency in mid-2018. China, however, has succeeded in its programme of technology transfer, overcoming obstacles that the Soviets weren't able to surmount.

* * *

The United States had an unfair advantage over the USSR in its post-war development. It suffered very little impact from the Second World War in terms of lives lost or infrastructure damaged; in fact, its manufacture of arms and supplies (including those supplied to the Nazi war machine) brought in handsome profits, along with the debt dependency it imposed on post-war Europe. All this meant that it was uniquely situated to invest massively in research and development, and to establish a very profitable domination over a large part of the developing world. Furthermore, via the so-called Washington Consensus, the United States established itself as the unchallenged leader of an international division of labour that brought economies of scale and a wide-ranging interchange of ideas in the worlds of science and culture.

In a useful article on the economic legacy of the October Revolution, Mark Buckley (2017) notes,

> In the post-World War II period, the capitalist world was reorganized and reintegrated under the leadership and dominance of the US. With many intervening twists and turns, that dominance later meant that in the 1980s the US was able to call on the surplus resources of the other capitalist powers in order to directly compete with the USSR – primarily using the savings of Japan. The chosen terrain of that competition was an arms race. The USSR lost the arms race in the way it would have lost almost any direct struggle with the US based on resources and technology, when the US integration in and dominance of the world market meant it was able to command vastly greater resources. . . .
>
> An emerging socialist society must participate in the international division of labour in order to survive and then prosper. . . . The Soviet Union could compete with the most advanced capitalist powers

> individually. But it could not compete when it cut itself off from world markets and they collaborated within world markets.

It is not fair to say that the USSR 'cut itself off from world markets' – in reality it was actively cut out of the international division of labour by the imperialist powers, in spite of the Soviet leadership's openly and often-stated desire to engage with the West on the basis of peace and equality. China from the late 1970s developed an incredibly sophisticated means of levering itself into the global economy and thereby absorbing the latest scientific and technological developments in record time, but the circumstances that enabled this may not have been available to the Soviet leaders. China was able to enjoy a more stable international environment; it withdrew to a significant degree from geopolitical confrontation with the United States; it was not expected to take military and financial responsibility for the entire socialist world; it could rely on the resources, goodwill and connections of an affluent and patriotic diaspora; and it could offer a vast pool of cheap labour to entice companies with cutting edge technology to invest in China. A China-style embrace of globalized knowledge may simply not have been available to the USSR.

* * *

One humdrum problem faced by Soviet citizens is that non-essential consumer goods and services were often either difficult to find or not terribly good quality (or both). As Kotz and Weir note, 'Many Soviet products, particularly consumer goods, were of low quality. Shoppers often faced long lines for ordinary goods in the notoriously inefficient system of retail distribution. Consumer services, from haircuts to appliance repair, were abysmal, if they were available at all.' This issue was partly related to an egalitarianism that aimed to produce low-cost goods in large numbers in order to make them widely accessible.

As such, everybody had food, clothes and housing, to go with the substantial social wage – education, healthcare, recreational facilities, libraries, and so on. Contrast this to Western capitalism, where rich people can enjoy unbelievable luxury while poor people struggle to feed their families.

However, the problem was also partly a function of the way the Soviet economy worked. Central planners could mandate the production of a million hair-dryers, but in the absence of competition and with a guaranteed market, there was little incentive for an enterprise to produce *good* hair-dryers. Hanson writes,

> Producers were concerned above all to meet targets set by planners. They had no particular reason to concern themselves with the wishes of the users of their products, nor with the activities of competitors. Indeed, the concept of competition was absent: other producers in the same line of activity were simply not competitors but fellow-executors of the state plan.

This was at a time when consumerism was reaching absurd new levels in the West. A combination of intense marketing, cut-throat competition, and the existence of credit-driven disposable income for significant sections of the population meant that middle-class people in the United States, Western Europe and Japan increasingly expected their hair-dryers and cars to be *lovely* rather than simply functional. Huge sums of money were being thrown at 'user-centred design' and similar concepts.

In the early post-war years, shoddy goods did not constitute the biggest problem for Soviet families, but expectations started to change, in no small part due to the increasing availability, penetration and sophistication of US propaganda. Many Soviet citizens felt envious of the consumer goods apparently enjoyed by people in the West, perhaps not always understanding that the idealized picture painted by the movies had its counterpart in horrific poverty, in the vulnerability of credit-driven consumption and in the ruthless domination of the neo-colonies by monopoly capital. The higher echelons of Soviet society – doctors, scientists, academics, bureaucrats – recognized that their counterparts in the West enjoyed a higher standard of living, and many started to feel that socialism was an obstacle to wealth.

In the grand scheme of things these should be fairly trivial concerns, but if a large section of the intelligentsia stops believing in the basic philosophical and economic underpinnings of society, this constitutes a quite serious problem for 'actually existing socialism' – a system which is always fragile in a historical epoch in which capitalism still dominates. Ideally, after half a century of socialist government, people would have developed a communist morality that was not much concerned with material wealth; but the experience of all socialist countries to date shows that breaking the cultural and ideological prejudices of thousands of years of class society is not something that can be achieved in the matter of a few years. Attempts to rapidly dismantle the cultural/ideological legacy of class society – most notably the Cultural Revolution in China – have not achieved their aims. Socialist society does not emerge 'on its own foundations, but, on the contrary', Marx wrote in 1875, 'from capitalist society'. It is therefore 'in every respect, economically, morally, and intellectually, still stamped with the birthmarks of the old society from whose womb it emerges'.

* * *

Poor quality of goods and services, along with shortages of key consumer goods and the repressed inflationary pressure of high wages, low prices and insufficient supply, all served to create a vibrant unofficial 'second economy', outside the central economic plan and therefore largely illegal. In a context where there is too much money chasing too few products, speculation and black-market activity become almost inevitable.

Because activity in the second economy was better rewarded than normal work, it served to undermine the rest of the economy. Parenti gives the following example, 'The poorer the restaurant service, the fewer the number of clients and the more food left over to take home for oneself or sell on the black market. The last thing restaurant personnel wanted was satisfied customers who would return to dine at the officially fixed low prices.'

Keeran and Kenny's *Socialism Betrayed* provides an authoritative description of the Soviet second economy and its knock-on effects,

> The second economy included the practices of managers reporting the loss or spoilage of goods in order to divert them to the black market. It embraced a common practice in state stores of salespeople and managers laying aside rare goods in order to secure tips from favoured customers or to sell them in the black market. Consumer durable goods like automobiles for which waiting lists existed presented 'considerable opportunity for graft', as well as for 'speculation', that is, for resale at higher prices. . . .
>
> Repairs, services and even production constituted other avenues of illegal gain. This included household repair, automotive repair, sewing and tailoring, moving furniture, and building private dwellings. This work, illegal in itself, often involved material and time stolen from regular employment. . . .
>
> The home production of grape and fruit wine and beer, the illegal resale of state beverages, and the sale of stolen ethanol accounted for as much as 2.2 per cent of the Gross Domestic Product in 1979.

Keeran and Kenny argue that the second economy reached a level where it created 'a layer of people who depended upon private activity for all or a substantial portion of their income' and that such people 'could rightly be considered a nascent class of petty bourgeoisie'. With the formation of an economic class comes the demand for political representation. Zyuganov writes that 'the shadow economy was running out of space for expanded reproduction; consequently, its bosses raised the question of how to weaken political restraints by influencing the state and Party apparatus, including the CPSU Central Committee, from the inside. It was under such pressures that perestroika came into existence.'

The growing second economy served to further reduce the effectiveness of the primary economy, contributing to shortages of goods and labour. All of this contributed to the undermining of Soviet socialism.

* * *

By the early 1980s, the USSR was dedicating vast resources to aiding socialist and progressive states around the world, most notably Vietnam, Cuba, Afghanistan, Ethiopia, Nicaragua, Angola and South Yemen. In many cases, such support was critical for the survival of these states. B.T. Ranadive (1987) of the CPI(M) correctly remarked that 'but for this help the economies of many newly liberated countries would have been helplessly dependent on Western aid'. The rising cost of this support – and particularly the waging of a long, difficult war in Afghanistan – coincided with the period of economic difficulties. Odd Arne Westad writes,

> The global role that the Soviets had taken on meant that both military expenditure – already in the late 1970s just slightly less than 25 per cent of GDP – and support for socialist states continued to increase into the 1980s, although it was clear to the leadership that the additional shortages this created at home were socially harmful and unpopular.

An anecdote reveals the dilemma for the Soviet leadership: Gerhard Schürer, head of the German Democratic Republic, appealed to Nikolai Baibakov for fuel in 1981. Baibakov's response is important. 'Should I cut back on oil to Poland? Vietnam is starving . . . should we just give away Southeast Asia? Angola, Mozambique, Ethiopia, Yemen . . . we carry them all. And our standard of living is extraordinarily low' (Friedman 2015).

In addition to the obvious economic cost, Soviet military support for its allies in Angola, Ethiopia and Afghanistan in particular were nails in the coffin of US–Soviet *detente*, and Cold War tensions reached new heights. The United States forced the USSR to divert huge resources into an 'arms race' that it could ill afford. Capitalism is actually far superior to socialism when it comes to the industry of death and destruction: in an economy aimed at furnishing profits for corporations, a large market for high-value single-use products like nuclear bombs is a wonderful thing, hence the position of the military-industrial complex at the heart of United States government. In an economy focused on serving the needs of the masses, devoting scarce resources to military technology means diverting resources away from producing food, housing, infrastructure, clothing, art, education and consumer goods.

* * *

By the early 1960s it was obvious to Soviet policymakers that the economy was in need of renovation. Growth rates at this point were still high, but agricultural production was insufficient. There were complaints about the quality and availability of goods, and the leadership was concerned about the continuing dependence on resource extraction for generating foreign exchange. Furthermore, the various 'hare-brained schemes, half-baked conclusions and hasty decisions' pursued by Nikita Khrushchev (Soviet leader from 1956 to 1964) had been singularly unsuccessful, leading his successors in the Brezhnev–Kosygin leadership to pursue a more conservative, less erratic, course of economic change.

In 1965, a fairly wide-ranging reform was introduced, designed principally by the economist Evsei Liberman and sponsored politically by Alexei Kosygin. The reform argued that the central planning system was becoming less effective and more expensive as economic relations became more complex. It sought to increase productivity, dynamism and growth. Enterprises were given greater autonomy over use of resources, and a concept of profitability was introduced. The wage levelling of the Khrushchev era was partially reversed, in an attempt to incentivize professional training. The reform included attempts to increase the use of computerization in planning, and to encourage technical innovation.

Controversially, the reform included some market measures, for example 'letting enterprise managers keep more of the return on their sales to the state and investing it in improving their machinery' and – as Aurthur wrote – allowing managers to 'spend more of this additional capital on material incentives for the production workers, to encourage them to cut waste, find hidden reserves of productivity in the existing machinery, and so forth'. The reform had some limited success, and growth in the second half of the 1960s (the beginning of the Brezhnev period) was higher than it had been in the first half (the end of the Khrushchev period). However, the positive effects did not last more than a few years, and it became clear that the Kosygin reforms had not resolved the underlying problems. A similar reform in the late 1970s had similarly uninspiring results.

A key issue was the absence of an effective feedback loop. The economic reforms launched by Deng Xiaoping in China in the late 1970s achieved infinitely greater success than anything the Soviets attempted. There are a number of reasons that China could succeed where the USSR failed in terms of renovating its economy, but one factor that stands out with the Chinese approach is the mantra of 'crossing the river by feeling the stones' – taking small steps, gathering feedback, learning lessons, and taking more steps. Allen Lynch writes that 'Deng pursued a strategy of incremental reforms in a pragmatic manner, building on economic success that he converted into political capital and gradually enlarging the reform process from farming to associated enterprises in the countryside, special economic zones along the southern coast and larger and larger regions of the country and sectors of the economy'. The Soviet approach was much more top-heavy.

Brezhnev died in November 1982, after 18 years as General Secretary of the Communist Party of the Soviet Union. The early period of his rule, from 1964 to around 1973, is generally considered as having been rather successful in terms of economic growth and geopolitical consolidation. After the economic experimentation, political instability and geostrategic brinkmanship of the Khrushchev era, the relatively conservative, steady leadership of Brezhnev and his team (including capable Marxists such as Andropov, Mikhail Suslov, Andrei Gromyko, Dmitriy Ustinov and Boris Ponomarev) reaped results. Quality of life increased; Soviet-supported national liberation movements overthrew colonial/neo-colonial powers; the threat of nuclear war with the United States seemed to wane a little. However, the period from the mid-1970s through to Brezhnev's death is widely regarded as the 'era of stagnation', reflected in a Politburo whose average age was pretty close to the prevailing Soviet life expectancy.

The election of KGB chief Yuri Andropov to CPSU General Secretary on November 12, 1982, inspired optimism. 'Andropov had admirable personal qualities, a solid grounding in Marxist-Leninist theory, rich leadership experience, a broad grasp of the problems facing the Soviet Union, and clear and forceful ideas about reform', write Keeran and Kenny. 'Under Brezhnev, when old age, infirmity, and laxness eroded Leninist norms among many at the top, Andropov lived modestly and gained a reputation as a workaholic.' Moreover, Andropov understood the need for systematic reform of the economy, particularly in clamping down on corruption, bringing in labour incentives, improving labour discipline, and modernizing production through the introduction of computer technology. He was also keen to improve Soviet democracy, through widened participation in management and decision making; although, unlike Gorbachev, he would never have attempted to weaken the CPSU or delegitimize its rule. In summary, Andropov seemed to understand the problems facing the Soviet Union and to have a sensible vision for addressing them.

Sadly, Andropov did not have time to turn his plans into reality. Only a few months after becoming General Secretary, he suffered renal failure. In August 1983 he was admitted into Moscow's Central Clinical Hospital, where he remained until his death on February 9, 1984. Andropov was succeeded by Konstantin Chernenko, who in the thirteen months before his own death did not show much of Andropov's vision and drive. Chernenko was succeeded by Mikhail Gorbachev.

* * *

> Given fifty or sixty years, we certainly ought to overtake the United States. This is an obligation. You have such a big population, such a vast territory and such rich resources, and what is more, you are said to be building socialism, which is supposed to be superior. If after working at it for fifty or sixty years you are still unable to overtake the United States, what a sorry figure you will cut!
>
> – Mao Zedong, 1956

Slow economic growth was not the central, direct cause of the Soviet Union's collapse. Even with sluggish growth, limited innovation and poor quality goods, the Soviet Union could have survived – plenty of countries in the world suffer these (and far worse) problems and remain relatively stable. But the economic problems fed into a general sentiment of dissatisfaction that reduced the masses' confidence in socialism and, therefore, their willingness to fight for it when it came under attack. The economic problems also created a stratum of people who felt they would do better under conditions of capitalism: people running small businesses in the informal sector who would benefit from freer markets; and managers and intellectuals who saw socialism as an impediment to a life of privilege.

Jude Woodward writes,

> It was the US's economic superiority, not its military threat, which eventually created the conditions for the defeat of the USSR. By the 1980s the USSR's economic problems meant it was impossibly squeezed by Reagan's new arms race. Rather than carry out a fundamental economic reform – as China had been doing for a decade – Gorbachev and then Yeltsin capitulated to the West, dissolved the Communist Party, accepted shock therapy and the break-up of the USSR.

CHAPTER 3

Decayed Confidence

Creating cohesive societies requires the cooperation of millions of people. Such levels of cooperation tend to rest upon shared systems of beliefs and values – whether implicit or explicit – that bind people to the existing social order. Modern capitalism, for example, is strongly rooted in individualism, consumerism, the cult of private property, the idea of the free market as being fundamental to human life, and a social hierarchy based on wealth. Feudalism, by contrast, has less emphasis on the freedom of the individual and its corresponding obsession with entrepreneurialism, and more emphasis on obedience to a king, lord, priest or other patriarch, whose absolute powers are implicitly bound up with those of a divine entity. This helps to explain, incidentally, the pervasiveness of strongly hierarchical religions in all feudal societies.

Collective belief in the values and foundational stories of a given society is a key survival factor for that society. This is why all societies go to great lengths to preserve these values and stories, to spread them through education and propaganda systems, and to present them as being universal and indisputable. Modern capitalism, with its extraordinarily powerful media and sophisticated means of propaganda, promotes its own beliefs and values, and we are exposed to these from the cradle to the grave.

The Soviet Union explicitly organized itself in accordance with a Marxist-Leninist ideology which emphasized values such as the common ownership of the means of production, peaceful development, internationalism, ending class divisions, and eliminating exploitation as well as social oppression. Lenin being Russian, Marxism-Leninism enjoyed an additional legitimacy among the Russians on account of its 'homegrown' status.

The early generations of Soviet people had a strong feeling that they were the vanguard of world revolution, of a bright new future. As they achieved the fastest industrialization in history, a precipitous improvement in the living standards of the masses, followed by the historic victory over fascism in the Second World War, the superiority of the Soviet system seemed assured. The spread of socialism to Europe, Asia and Cuba in the 1940s and '50s also fed into this feeling, as did the rise of the national liberation movements across Africa.

The immediate post-war years – with fascism defeated thanks to the heroism of the Soviet people, with the Cold War yet to make its full impact, and with a national leader (Stalin) who was very widely respected – probably constitute the zenith of Soviet pride and national spirit. Through the 1960s, 1970s and 1980s, however, more and more people lost their commitment to the official ruling ideology; society's foundational stories were starting to lose their pull. By the time the Communist Party leadership itself started (under Gorbachev) to challenge the basic beliefs underlying the system, the masses were by and large sufficiently alienated from these beliefs that they were ambivalent in the face of this cyclopean act of social sabotage.

* * *

> We will not do to Chairman Mao what Khrushchev did to Stalin.
>
> – Deng Xiaoping

After a lengthy and complicated power struggle between Nikita Khrushchev and Georgy Malenkov following Stalin's death (in March 1953), Khrushchev had managed to consolidate power towards the end of 1955. One of his first priorities was to attack Stalin's legacy in relation to excessive political repression, abuse of power, mass deportations, and the cult of the personality. His 'secret speech' at the 20th Congress of the CPSU in February 1956 is a watershed moment in Soviet history.

According to Khrushchev and his allies, the speech was not intended to entirely negate Stalin. The speech starts by noting that 'the role of Stalin in the preparation and execution of the Socialist Revolution, in the Civil War, and in the fight for the construction of socialism in our country, is universally known'. It ends by admitting that 'Stalin undoubtedly performed great services to the Party, to the working class and to the international workers' movement'. Rather, Khrushchev's professed purpose was to expose Stalin's errors and excesses with a view to improving and modernizing the Soviet political system – doing away with personality cults and establishing a coherent system of socialist revolutionary legality.

To what extent some level of 'destalinization' was needed at that time remains a controversial and difficult topic on the left. The fact that the CPSU leadership went along with Khrushchev's line indicates that there was a fairly widespread feeling that the repression under Stalin had been excessive and that there was a need to create a more relaxed political environment.

Yet this same leadership had supported Stalin when he was alive. This disparity can at least be partly explained by the fast-changing political environment. Harsh repression and the personality cult both had their roots in political necessity, in a context where the young Soviet state was desperately struggling for its life. Unattractive as it may be, any socialist revolution requires repression in order not to be overthrown by its internal and external enemies. As Engels famously wrote in his article *On Authority* (1872),

> A revolution is certainly the most authoritarian thing there is; it is the act whereby one part of the population imposes its will upon the other part by means of rifles, bayonets and cannon – authoritarian means, if such there be at all; and if the victorious party does not want to have fought

> in vain, it must maintain this rule by means of the terror which its arms inspire in the reactionists. Would the Paris Commune have lasted a single day if it had not made use of this authority of the armed people against the bourgeois? Should we not, on the contrary, reproach it for not having used it freely enough?

Having seized power, the Soviet working class found itself having to contend with a ruthless and well-connected former elite, a peasant majority that was a long way from being a stable ally, and an intelligentsia that was largely suspicious and disparaging of the upstart Bolsheviks. Lenin and his comrades had been convinced that the Russian Revolution would help to spark a series of socialist revolutions throughout the continent, thereby replacing powerful European enemies with powerful European allies. This European revolution failed to materialize. Instead of the European working class coming to the aid of its Soviet brothers and sisters, the European *ruling* classes came to the aid of the White Army of deposed capitalists and landowners in order to destroy the Soviet project. The Soviet state was forced to withstand a bloody civil war, followed by an extensive programme of sanctions, espionage and destabilization conducted by the Western powers and Japan throughout the 1920s and '30s; and finally, the genocidal war and horrific devastation wrought by the Nazis. Clearly, the USSR would not have survived without repression, and it is not particularly difficult to understand how this repression could have gone out of control.

Michael Parenti (2001) describes the practical inevitability of an over-centralized state in a socialist country struggling to preserve its existence and independence in a hostile imperialist world:

> For a people's revolution to survive, it must seize state power and use it to (a) break the stranglehold exercised by the owning class over the society's institutions and resources, and (b) withstand the reactionary

counterattack that is sure to come. The internal and external dangers a revolution faces necessitate a centralized state power that is not particularly to anyone's liking, not in Soviet Russia in 1917, nor in Sandinista Nicaragua in 1980.

Szymanski (1979) contextualizes the harsh features of the Stalin-era Soviet state as follows:

> The policies in the period of Stalin's leadership, as well as the mechanisms for decision making and mass involvement, were dictated in their broad outlines by the situation and were not the product of Stalin's personal motives or psychological state. On the contrary, the personalities and motives of Stalin and the other leaders were socially formed according to the requirements of the situation, and the leadership itself was socially selected on the basis of the effects of these two elements. . . . The process of socialist transformation is not the best of all possible worlds; in fact it is simply the necessary stage to create such a world – communism. As a result, some people unjustly suffer and there are negative consequences of otherwise positive developments. Abuses of the personality cult and the danger of arbitrary decision making were the most serious of these negative consequences.

Even the personality cult served a purpose,

> The personality cult around Stalin (and that around Lenin) served the function of winning the support of the peasantry and the new working class. In lieu of the peasants' fundamental involvement in making the socialist revolution, the Bolshevik regime had to be personalized for it to win their loyalty. Even in China and Cuba, where there was authentic massive peasant support, the charisma of Mao and Fidel have played important roles. . . . The personality cult serves a key social function when circumstances don't allow for the much slower development of the

class-conscious understanding and struggle needed to win people to a socialism without individual heroes.

Szymanski explores this question further in his 1984 book *Human Rights in the Soviet Union*:

> The 'cult of personality' served the vital social function of symbolizing the unity and solidarity of Soviet society, a unity and solidarity essential in the 1930s and 1940s, and that could best be quickly created by personalizing it in the form of the celebration of a single individual 'father figure' who was portrayed in a Christ-like fashion as omniscient and benevolent. The cult of Stalin, in fact, took on many of the characteristics of the Russian Orthodox religion, that was the easiest route for the Party to follow in order to secure legitimacy among peasants and ex-peasants.

Khrushchev himself recognized that the deficiencies of the political apparatus in the Stalin era did not arise out of madness or malice but out of a commitment to the working class and the struggle for socialism, 'We cannot say that these were the deeds of a giddy despot. Stalin considered that this should be done in the interest of the Party, of the working masses, in the name of the defence of the revolution's gains' (quoted in Smith 2014).

That aside, personality cults and excessive centralization of power constitute distortions and they bring their own dangers. Relatively crude political measures were surely a necessary response to the real threats faced by the nascent socialist state, but they could not but have a detrimental long-term effect, and therefore it was important to make political changes when circumstances allowed. B.T. Ranadive (1987) writes,

> The conditions under which power was captured and the continuing resistance of the exploiting classes, helped from abroad, demanded strict

> punitive measures. It is now known that these were continued even when the situation ceased to warrant them. . . . The cult of personality under Stalin and Mao led to the erosion of inner-party democracy, and also complicated the relationship between the party and the masses.

In the changed political context of the post-war years, there was a good case for doing away with personality cults, widening popular democracy, increasing freedom of public debate, extending individual liberties, and building new norms of socialist legality. At the subjective level, changes were obviously needed in order to restore revolutionary optimism. Soviet society was by now in its second or third generation, forty years removed from the uprising of the St Petersburg metalworkers. The expectations of workers in the 1950s were significantly different to the expectations of the first generation of Soviet revolutionaries.

External circumstances supported a loosening of the political system. The USSR was no longer isolated: the socialist camp had expanded to include a large part of Asia and Europe, and important countries such as India and Indonesia had broken free from the grip of European colonialism and were being transformed into independent powers, more or less friendly towards the Soviet Union. The country's vast borders were less vulnerable now that they were now largely shared with friendly states: China, Mongolia, DPR Korea, Poland, Romania, Czechoslovakia and Afghanistan. Meanwhile, the arrival of the era of nuclear weapons meant that both the USSR and USA had more to lose from outright war between the two superpowers; *peaceful coexistence* became plausible, indeed necessary.

Szymanski (1984) notes that, by the middle of 1953,

> An armistice was finally signed in the Korean War. In 1954 the Geneva Agreements ending the war in Indochina were signed. In 1955, the first summit meeting since 1945 was held between the top leaders of the USSR

> and the Western powers, and the treaty permanently neutralizing Austria and providing for the withdrawal of Western and Soviet troops was signed. Peaceful co-existence was in the air and the pressure on the Soviet Union was relaxed. No more under a state of external siege as intense as that in the 1928–53 period, the level of political repression in Soviet society never again approached the level of those years. Further, with socialist reconstruction and collectivization complete, and a high level of legitimacy of the Soviet system achieved, never again was there the extraordinary need for domestic mobilization or for deliberate creation of unifying symbols such as had existed over the previous 25 years of almost permanent crisis.

So, it is reasonable to assume that Khrushchev's criticism of Stalin was motivated by a desire to introduce progressive political changes consistent with developing socialism in new circumstances. His methods, however, were disastrous. It should have been possible to make political changes without launching a severe frontal attack on Stalin and all that he represented. Stalin was the most prominent Soviet leader from 1924 until his death in 1953. In other words, Stalin led the USSR for twenty-nine of the thirty-six years of the USSR's existence. To criticize him so harshly, to tear down a personality cult so suddenly, meant to cast doubt on the entire Soviet experience to that point; it meant to delegitimize the extraordinary achievements of the CPSU and the Soviet people during the Stalin era. Even Vladislav Zubok – an anti-Stalinist by any measure – observes that '*the destruction of Stalin's cult wounded the Soviet ideological consensus*'.

The situation demanded a more balanced, nuanced assessment of the Stalin period (although we should note in passing that, even now, such a thing is rare). The post-Mao leadership in China had criticisms of Mao that were not entirely dissimilar to the Khrushchev leadership's criticisms of Stalin. Some of the changes they introduced had parallels with those envisaged by Khrushchev. And yet it did not occur to the

Chinese leadership to try to destroy Mao's legacy. Deng Xiaoping made an insightful comment on this subject in an interview given to the Italian journalist Oriana Fallaci in 1980,

> We will make an objective assessment of Chairman Mao's contributions and his mistakes. We will reaffirm that his contributions are primary and his mistakes secondary. We will adopt a realistic approach towards the mistakes he made late in life. We will continue to adhere to Mao Zedong Thought, which represents the correct part of Chairman Mao's life. Not only did Mao Zedong Thought lead us to victory in the revolution in the past; it is – and will continue to be – a treasured possession of the Chinese Communist Party and of our country. That is why we will forever keep Chairman Mao's portrait on Tiananmen Gate as a symbol of our country, and we will always remember him as a founder of our Party and state. . . . *We will not do to Chairman Mao what Khrushchev did to Stalin.*

Nearly four decades later, Mao's portrait still occupies pride of place on Tiananmen Gate.

Khrushchev's speech created widespread confusion and doubt; anger, in some places. A report from 2015 on a recently rebuilt statue of Stalin in the village of Eski Ikan, Kazakhstan, contains a thought-provoking quote from a Second World War veteran who, along with his fellow villagers, had resisted attempts by the local authorities to dismantle Stalin's statue in the late 1950s in the wake of Khrushchev's speech,

> We fought the Nazis with the battle cry 'For the Homeland! For Stalin!', and they wanted to pull down the statue. Over our dead bodies, we said. We stood firm, and we won. ('Villagers put Stalin back on pedestal', 2015)

The post-Khrushchev leadership of Brezhnev and his team (from 1964) rolled back the attack on Stalin's legacy settling on a more balanced assessment that emphasized Stalin's historic role in guiding the construction of Soviet socialism and leading the war effort, whilst decrying abuses of power. However, the first steps towards undermining Soviet ideology had been taken, and these laid the ground for the generation of right-wing and liberal intellectuals who, in the Gorbachev era, made their way to the heart of government and led the dismantling of socialism.

* * *

The adverse effects of Khrushchev's speech were felt beyond the borders of the USSR. The British Marxist historian Eric Hobsbawm wrote that 'to put it in the simplest terms, the October Revolution created a world communist movement, the 20th Congress destroyed it'.

In truth, significant cracks had been observable in the world communist movement for quite some time. Failing to understand the strategic necessity of the non-aggression pact signed between Germany and the Soviet Union in August 1939 (incorrectly perceiving it as a capitulation to fascism, rather than an unavoidable act of self-defence forced on the USSR by Western Europe's accommodation of Hitler and its desire to push Germany into attacking the USSR), Communist parties in Europe and the Americas suffered deep divisions and waves of resignations. Many longstanding communists who had fought against fascism in the streets of London or Paris – or in the Jarama valley – felt confused and betrayed, and the local communist leaderships struggled to promote solidarity with the Soviet Union whilst simultaneously maintaining the fight against fascism on the ground.

Further confusion, disunity and disillusion was created when the Soviet leadership advised the French and Italian Communist parties not to attempt armed revolutionary uprisings in the late 1940s. This advice was given on the basis of level-headed strategic reasoning about the relative balance of forces in Europe (most importantly the permeation of US troops in western Europe and the inability of the Soviet Union to provide direct military support to those countries); however, it generated resentment and divisions that would grow and spawn further problems in the decades to come.

In the early post-war period, serious disagreements emerged between the Yugoslav and Soviet Communist parties over a number of issues: the establishment of a stable peace in Europe, the possibilities for supporting the communist side in the Greek Civil War, and the economic mechanisms of building socialism in Eastern Europe. Whichever side was right or wrong in the initial disagreements, the Soviet leadership responded to Yugoslavia's assertion of independence in a heavy-handed way that served to inspire distrust of the USSR. As Szymanski (1979) described it,

> The Soviets, in March 1948, began taking strong sanctions against Yugoslavia. On March 18 all Soviet military advisers were withdrawn, and on March 19 all economic advisers. An embargo was placed on trade with Yugoslavia by the Soviet Union and all the other socialist countries. This threatened the collapse of the Yugoslav economy, which was heavily dependent on trade with the East European countries because of the West's hostility to recent Yugoslav nationalizations and the friendly relations since 1945 among the East European countries. The Yugoslav Communist Party was expelled from the world communist movement and its leaders compared to fascists. Leading communists were put on trial throughout Eastern Europe and charged with treason for being Titoists. The Soviets also tried to overthrow Tito's leadership inside his own country by supporting alternative leadership within the Yugoslav Party. Although never carried out, the Soviets also made threats of military intervention against Yugoslavia.

Yugoslavia was by no means an insignificant country, and Tito and the Yugoslav Communist Party had earned enormous respect around the world for their heroic defence against Nazi occupation. Tito had been known to many European communists and anti-fascists before the Second World War, when he managed the Paris centre recruiting anti-fascist volunteers to fight in the Spanish Civil War. The Yugoslavs' sudden expulsion from the Information Bureau of the Communist and Workers' Parties (*Cominform*, established in 1947 in order to coordinate actions between Communist parties, and which ironically was headquartered in Belgrade) and the severe measures taken against it shocked many people in the West European parties.

The unity of the world communist movement was even more profoundly shaken by the Sino-Soviet split, which started to quietly emerge in 1957 and which by the early 1960s became a full-scale ideological conflict. Initially, Mao Zedong and his comrades had cautiously welcomed Khrushchev's policies of destalinization and peaceful coexistence; but from 1957, driven in part by a resentment of Soviet hegemonism and in part by their own turn towards a more radical domestic agenda (particularly the Great Leap Forward, which represented a major break with the economic programme proposed by the Soviets), they started to voice their opposition to these policies. The Soviets over-reacted to the questioning of their authority over the global communist movement, and punished China by unilaterally withdrawing their thousands of advisers and by criticizing Chinese ultra-leftism in international forums. The Chinese side took to increasingly bitter polemics against Soviet revisionism, actively challenging the USSR's leadership of the global communist movement.

By the mid-1960s, with Mao preparing his last and most extreme campaign against what he considered capitalist roaders in China, what became the Cultural Revolution, the Chinese came to define the Soviet Union as a capitalist country that had capitulated entirely to US imperialism. Increasingly, the Chinese Communist Party based its relations with foreign Communist parties on the basis of their willingness to denounce the Soviet Union. From this point, practically every country outside the socialist camp had mutually hostile pro-Moscow and pro-Beijing Communist parties. Odd Arne Westad observes that the split 'made it possible to tack between the two self-proclaimed centres of communism and get support from both, but it also signalled an internal split in many parties, which in some cases reduced them to political irrelevance (if not infantility)'.

Soviet prestige – and, presumably, self-esteem – was much affected by China's loud denunciations, particularly in relation to Soviet support for national liberation struggles. The USSR prided itself on giving extensive support to fraternal countries and parties (not least China, which was the recipient of an extraordinary level of aid from the USSR between 1950 and 1959), but its support for military struggles against imperialism was limited by its desire not to incite any wider conflict with the US. Although 'peaceful coexistence' was presented by the Chinese as an example of Khrushchev's revisionism and capitulation to capitalism, in reality it was an extension of the post-war *realpolitik* that emphasized the need for peace, stability, security and recovery. Canadian political analyst Stephen Gowans (2012) writes,

> The USSR desperately needed space to develop its economy, free from the continual threat of military aggression from the United States and its NATO allies. . . . The Soviet Union could ill afford a war with the Americans, and Stalin therefore refused to support revolutionary movements in his allies' sphere of influence and acted with caution in supporting revolutionary movements elsewhere. There is a considerable continuity in Stalin's efforts to keep the hostility of capitalist powers at bay, and Khrushchev's call for peaceful coexistence.

Increasingly, the Chinese Communist Party was able to point to lukewarm Soviet support to militant national liberation movements as proof that the USSR had given up on the fight against imperialism and that China was the natural leader of the global anti-imperialist struggle. This argument resonated in much of Asia, Africa and Latin America.

The Sino-Soviet split also opened a path for the United States to 'triangulate' in its war on the socialist camp, siding with one against the other in order to avoid facing a united socialist bloc.

After taking power in 1964, the Brezhnev leadership stepped up Soviet solidarity with national liberation movements and the post-colonial states of Africa, and Soviet prestige on the international stage also benefited from the chaos that reigned in the Chinese Foreign Ministry in the late 1960s during the Cultural Revolution. However, the Soviet Union would never regain its place as the undisputed leader of the oppressed masses of the world. Jeremy Friedman writes that 'revolutionary energies exploded in the developing world. The grievances that motivated these revolutionary outbreaks were often expressed in terms of identity – racial, ethnic, or national – more than class, while in the industrialized world the insurrectionary ferment of the now largely sated working class was replaced by the alienation of students and racial minorities.' The Soviet Union was less experienced in dealing with these movements than it was with the traditional organizations of the industrial working class, and Soviet socialism had a less obvious appeal for them.

The interventions of the USSR and its allies to quell uprisings in Hungary (1956) and Czechoslovakia (1968) had a further detrimental effect on popular opinion of the Soviet Union. In both cases, Soviet intervention served to prevent the overthrow of socialist governments by an unholy alliance of social democrats, liberals, religious fundamentalists and fascists (financed and mobilized in part from Wall Street); nevertheless, they inevitably lent legitimacy to Cold War accusations of a 'communist empire'. Even within the left, these interventions were highly controversial. One reflection of the trajectory of the Sino-Soviet split is that the Chinese strongly encouraged Khrushchev to intervene in Hungary in 1956, but then denounced the intervention in Czechoslovakia as an example of 'social imperialism'. In terms of the reaction of the Western Communist parties, Friedman writes that the Czech crisis led these parties 'to decide that their chances of political success did not lie along the road laid out by Moscow'.

Whereas the Soviet Union in the 1920s and '30s had been the apple of the eye of the global working-class movement, by the late 1960s it was viewed in a negative light by many of the progressive elements outside the socialist camp – due to the various issues outlined above, and also to the extraordinary intensity of Cold War propaganda and McCarthyite repression from the late 1940s onwards. When hundreds of thousands came out into the streets in 1968 in Paris and elsewhere, they certainly did not carry portraits of Leonid Brezhnev. As Westad wrote,

> The Western European and American students who demonstrated in the streets and occupied their universities in the late 1960s found the 'old' Left – both socialists and Communists – too timid on domestic reform and too placid in dealing with the problems of the Third World. Only 'direct action' from below, through an alliance of students and workers, could break the impasse in Western politics, the New Left radicals believed. The NLF [National Liberation Front of Vietnam] or Che Guevara – or even China's Cultural Revolution – became symbols of the impassioned action demanded by student protesters. 'The Third World taught us the concept of an uncompromising and radical policy, different from the shallow, unprincipled bourgeois Realpolitik,' Hans-Jürgen Krahl, one of the leaders of the West Berlin student revolt, told his judges from the dock in 1968. 'Che Guevara, Fidel Castro, Ho Chi Minh, and Mao Zedong are revolutionaries who teach us the political ethics of the uncompromising policy, which enables us to do two things: first, to reject the policies of peaceful coexistence, such as is being conducted as Realpolitik by the Soviet Union, and, second, to see clearly the terror that the United States,

assisted by the Federal Republic of Germany, is carrying out in the Third World.'

The unstoppable tide of progressive opinion in the West away from Soviet-style socialism even prompted many of the CPSU's closest allies in Western Europe to distance themselves from Moscow, cultivating a variety of socialism they hoped would be more palatable to Western tastes and which emphasized ideological independence from the Soviet Union.

* * *

Jeremy Friedman, in *Shadow Cold War*, writes,

> As the world sank into depression and politics radicalized across the ideological spectrum in the 1930s, the prospect of working-class revolution in the industrialized nations, where traditional Marxism had always envisioned it, seemed very real indeed. With bread lines, mass unemployment, and violent, racist, authoritarian politics the order of the day in much of Europe and North America, the explosive economic growth of Stalin's USSR seemed to provide a tempting alternative. By the 1960s, though, the global revolutionary battleground had shifted. The West, to the shock not only of Moscow, but of many in Washington and London as well, had failed to return to depression after the war, and the prospects for Marxist revolution in the developed world began to recede.

The onset of the Great Depression, which lasted from 1929 until the outbreak of the Second World War in 1939, led Soviet economists to conclude that the Western capitalist countries had entered a period of 'general crisis'. They theorized that this crisis had pushed capitalism into terminal decline and would therefore ignite a global shift to socialism. The general crisis, noted a Soviet textbook from 1954, 'embraces an entire period of history, in the course of which take place the breakdown of capitalism and victory of socialism on a world scale. . . . While the capitalist system becomes more and more entangled in insoluble contradictions, the socialist system develops on a steadily upward-moving line, without crises and catastrophes.' The general crisis meant that capitalism had lost its economic vigour and would no longer be able to innovate; it was no longer capable of generating progress, of developing the productive force. 'A characteristic feature of the general crisis of capitalism is chronic under-capacity working of enterprises and chronic mass unemployment.'

This theory, voiced with such certainty by Soviet economists and their global allies, must have seemed like an absolute truth in the 1930s, when the Soviet economy was growing at five per cent a year while in the US output *fell by 30 per cent* and unemployment *increased eightfold*, from three per cent to 24 per cent (figures from Ha-Joon Chang 2014). And yet the theory of the general crisis severely underestimated post-war capitalism's ability to cheat death. The Soviet Union won the Second World War, but in so doing it sustained the most horrific human and economic losses. The United States, meanwhile, had been able to attach itself to the winning side and turn a handsome profit at the same time.

Separated from the main theatres of war by the Atlantic and Pacific oceans, the United States emerged from the war with comparatively little destruction and loss of life. As a result, by the time the war ended in 1945 it was far and away the strongest economic power, and it leveraged this power to establish hegemony over a new capitalist order. Jude Woodward notes that

> The US had a good war; as a result of vast state investment to deliver the materials and goods needed for war, its economy doubled in size between 1939 and 1944. In 1945 its economy was larger than the sum of all 29 countries of Western Europe as well as Japan, Canada, New Zealand and

> Australia; and it was only marginally smaller than all these and the USSR. Its share of industrial production was even greater. And the bombs that fell on Hiroshima and Nagasaki had announced it as the greatest military power yet seen on Earth.

Five years later, in 1950, as Westad notes, its GDP 'was higher than all of Europe's put together, and possibly equal to that of Europe plus the Soviet Union'.

Enormous investment in Western Europe via the Marshall Plan provided lucrative avenues of investment for US capital, whilst establishing a solid anti-communist bloc to counter the huge prestige of the Soviet Union, and creating an economic bond that would force Western Europe to unite behind US leadership. The establishment of the North Atlantic Treaty Organization (NATO) added a military factor to this new-found imperialist unity, and the Bretton Woods system instituted an international monetary order that was controlled almost exclusively by the US.

In short, the US was able to breathe new life into global capitalism after the Second World War by using its economic dominance to reduce inter-imperialist rivalry, give a kick-start to economic globalization, introduce some Keynesian reforms, prevent several countries from adopting socialism (via bribery, coups and/or military intervention), and unite efforts to isolate and destabilize the socialist camp. As a result, far from languishing in a 'general crisis', monopoly capitalism entered something of a golden era, during which it was able to realize undeniable advances in science and technology, as well as raise living standards and create opportunities for large sections of the population.

In the Soviet Union it had been taken for granted that, with the defeat of fascism and the continuing economic crisis and political disunity in Europe, the socialist path would become irresistible. Khrushchev turned the idea of 'catching up with and surpassing America' into a national obsession. In China, Mao framed the Great

Leap Forward in terms of 'closing the gap between China and the US within five years, and to ultimately surpass the US within seven years'. This was a rather drastic raise on his bid just a few months earlier to catch up with Britain within 15 years (this latter goal was in fact achieved a bit later than planned, in 2005, using economic methods somewhat different to those envisioned by the Great Helmsman).

In retrospect, these goals created unrealistic expectations, which ended up feeding resentment and disappointment. More appropriate objectives might have focused on a broader concept of human development, along with a longer-term strategy for technological competitiveness. Nevertheless, the idea of 'catching up with and surpassing America' was not as hair-brained as it might seem now. 'Positing alternative US growth rates of 2.5, 3 and 4 per cent per annum, and Soviet growth rates of 6, 7 and 8 per cent, they generated nine catch-up dates. The earliest was 1973, the latest 1996', notes Hanson (2014). 'Hypothetical though the exercise was, the fact that it was conducted at all, and the range of Soviet growth rates chosen, reveal that Khrushchev's talk of catching-up did not at the time seem entirely ridiculous.'

And yet closing the gap proved difficult. The United States had a number of advantages that enabled it to sustain steady growth throughout the 1950s and 1960s: unlike the Soviet Union, it was not devastated by war; unlike in the Soviet Union, wars and military expenditure constituted an economic boost rather than a drain; unlike the Soviet Union, it benefited immensely from the exploitation of people and resources in the developing world; and unlike the Soviet Union, it felt no particular obligation to privilege the basic needs of the masses over the exploration of new markets and technologies.

Furthermore, the other countries in the capitalist camp were for the most part advanced industrialized economies, and their integration into a bloc provided an important impulse for scientific collaboration. Meanwhile, the countries newly incorporated into the socialist camp were the poorer and less-developed countries of Eastern and Central Europe, along with the barely (if at all) industrialized nations of East Asia.

But once an expectation is set, the failure to meet it creates disappointment. The Soviet Union continued to grow at an impressive rate well into the 1970s, but so did the United States and the major economies of Western Europe and Japan; therefore, the gap did not close. By the late 1970s, Soviet growth was grinding to a halt, just as the United States and Western Europe were starting to dial up their attacks on the organized working class, privatizing, globalizing, deregulating, lowering wages, and leveraging technology to stimulate a redefined economy with the balance of power tipped even further in favour of the capitalist class.

With the gap in living standards between the US and USSR growing wider, frustration started to take hold in the socialist countries since, as Deng Xiaoping pointed out in 1984, '*the superiority of the socialist system is demonstrated, in the final analysis, by faster and greater development of the productive forces than under the capitalist system*'.

* * *

> Why did the Soviet Union disintegrate? Why did the Soviet Communist Party collapse? An important reason was that their ideals and beliefs had been shaken.
>
> – Xi Jinping

As it became increasingly clear that US-led Western capitalism was *not* on the verge of collapse; as the CPSU started to lose its undisputed leadership role in the global movement for a better world; and as the Soviet economy started to show signs of old age, nihilism began to creep into the popular mindset. The official line found in the pages of the Party's newspapers and textbooks was that the plan remained on track – that the Soviet economy was going from strength to strength and that imperialism was wheezing its way to a long-overdue death. This narrative simply did not ring true to a lot of people. Rather than presenting and attempting to explain the changed global situation, the Party increasingly found itself shouting slogans that were out of touch with reality.

Keeran and Kenny (2004) observe that 'in many respects ideology became complacent, formalized, and ritualistic. As a result, ideology repelled many of the best and brightest'. Some of the more astute theoreticians within the Soviet leadership – people such as Mikhail Suslov and Boris Ponomarev – worked to adapt Marxism-Leninism to the new circumstances of the 1960s and '70s, indicating that the Party at least acknowledged the growing problems of ideological stultification and popular alienation. However, these efforts did not have the desired effect. The CPSU's ideology was never able to recover the relevance, urgency, utility and currency that it enjoyed in the pre-war era.

A number of other factors fed into this. For one thing, Soviet society had become more open to external influence. US propaganda was more sophisticated and easily available than ever before. Broadcasts from *Voice of America* were directed to the USSR from 1947. The VOA and other radio stations worked feverishly to destabilize Soviet society, painting a rosy picture of life in the West whilst at the same time exaggerating the extent of the problems faced by the USSR. Khrushchev had also introduced a cultural 'thaw' which saw an increase in the number of foreign books, movies and records, and which allowed an unprecedented level of open criticism of the state by Soviet writers. This was most famously manifested in Khrushchev's personal approval of the publication of *One Day in the Life of Ivan Denisovich*, a much-sensationalized account of life in Soviet prisons, written by the obsessively anti-communist tsarism-nostalgist Aleksandr Solzhenitsyn. Furthermore, with the *detente*, more Soviet citizens travelled to Western Europe and North America, and were able to witness a material standard of living that was significantly more comfortable than they experienced at home. Over half a century later, it is difficult to judge the extent to which the 'thaw' was a mistake on Khrushchev's part or a more or less inevitable response to the popular demand for a more open society at that time. The need to widen democracy and allow greater individual freedoms is a complex problem for socialist states under siege. In a world dominated by imperialism, a socialist leadership has to carefully balance responding to the legitimate demands and needs of the people with not creating structures that can easily be leveraged by hostile states to destabilize and to spread disinformation. Khrushchev likely went too far without a parallel campaign to promote Soviet advances and values. The Brezhnev leadership partially reversed the 'thaw', but by that point the critics of the system had established themselves as personalities, had built a following, and were in contact with one another; driven underground, the 'thaw' transformed into a dissident movement that would become a major *cause célèbre* in the West and served to further undermine the confidence and prestige of the Soviet people. No simultaneous attempt was created to champion Soviet values.

Another problem faced by all socialist societies (at least, all those that survive longer than a single generation) is how to maintain revolutionary zeal through multiple generations. The average Soviet citizen of 1967 was a very different person from the average Soviet citizen of 1917; she had an entirely different experience of life and understanding of the world, along with different expectations, motivations and aspirations. She hadn't been inspired directly by the steelworkers standing up defiantly against ruthless bosses or the humble peasants demanding land and peace. Her education told her that the struggle against capitalism and for socialism was important, but she had not necessarily learnt it from life experience in the same way that her parents or grandparents had. So how can she be persuaded to fight like they did? This remains a tough problem for the socialist world to solve; after all, what revolution thus far can claim that its second or third generation has been able to match the revolutionary passion of its first generation? The Soviet leadership attempted to dodge this particular bullet by maintaining power largely in the hands of the earlier generation of revolutionaries and, particularly in the Brezhnev period, keeping people in top positions for longer rather than seeking to introduce younger people. The average age of Politburo members rose from 55 in 1966 to 68 in 1982 (Curtis 1998). This clearly contributed to the ideological alienation of young people.

Chinese scholar Hu Yanxin put forward five propositions on the failure of CPSU propaganda in this era (cited in Shambaugh 2008):

1. Propaganda was tedious in content, monotonous in form, and disconnected from reality.
2. The authorities concealed the truth by only reporting good news, which lost the people's trust.
3. The CPSU dealt with intellectual circles by administrative and repressive means.
4. Real information had to come from abroad, but this only made Russians further disbelieve their own media.
5. The CPSU failed to accurately analyse the new changes in the West objectively, thus losing the opportunity to develop in line with the new scientific and technological revolution.

With a declining communist and collectivist mentality, a capitalist and individualist mentality reappeared quickly to fill the gap, fuelled by Western propaganda and by the habits preserved in the social fabric through many centuries of class society pre-1917. Yuri Andropov somewhat wistfully observed,

> The people who have accomplished a socialist revolution have for a long

> time yet fully to grasp their new position as supreme and undivided owners of all public wealth – to grasp it economically, politically and, if you wish, psychologically, developing a collectivist mentality and behaviour. . . . Even when socialist production relations are finally established, some people preserve, and even reproduce individualist habits, a striving to profit at others' expense, at the expense of society. All this, to use Marx's terminology, are consequences of the alienation of labour and they do not automatically and suddenly evaporate from the mind, although alienation itself has already been abolished.

The sections of the population most affected by disillusion and ideological deterioration were academics, managers and Party bureaucrats – the 'party-state elite', as Kotz and Weir refer to them. Not only were they more aware than others of how the country's economic position was declining vis-à-vis the West, but they had to suffer in the knowledge that their counterparts enjoyed far greater perks and privileges. A Soviet factory worker enjoyed far greater prestige than his Western counterpart and had a comparable quality of life; even with a less varied diet and lower quality consumer goods, he or she had access to a comprehensive social welfare system that the US could not compete with. A scientist, university lecturer or technocrat, on the other hand, could feel decidedly resentful at her relative impecuniosity:

> Despite the material benefits accruing to the elite, those benefits paled by comparison to the material advantages enjoyed by their counterparts in the elite of the Western capitalist countries. . . . The Soviet system had a much smaller gap between the top and bottom of the income distribution than do capitalist systems. The general director of a large Soviet enterprise was paid about four times as much as the average industrial wage. By contrast, the average American corporate chief executive officer's pay is nearly 150 times that of the average factory worker. (Kotz and Weir 1997)

Such people stood to gain from a transition to capitalism. Capitalism would allow them unchallenged ownership of the means of production; it would give them the opportunity to accumulate enormous wealth without having to worry about attracting unwanted attention from the state. Furthermore, this wealth could be legally passed on to their children.

In a context of rising alienation, economic stagnation and ideological deterioration, it was easy enough for the seeds of counter-revolution to sprout.

CHAPTER 4

Imperialist Destabilization

Not for a moment since 1917 have the fascist and democratic Western powers abandoned the idea of defeating the Soviet Union.

– Samir Amin

Seeing the Soviet Union experiencing economic and political difficulties, and noting the deepening split within the socialist camp, strategists in the West perceived a potentially historic opportunity to push the USSR off the cliff. From the late 1970s, the Western ruling class pursued this track relentlessly: rolling back *detente*, expanding sanctions, massively increasing spending on military technology, and drawing the Soviet Union deeper and deeper into war in Afghanistan. As Yuri Andropov recognized in 1982, 'The more warlike factions in the West have become very active, their class-based hatred of socialism prevailing over considerations of realism and sometimes over plain common sense. . . . They are trying to win military superiority over the USSR, over all the countries of the socialist community.'

Inaugurated as US president in January 1981, the ultra-conservative Ronald Reagan launched a 'full-court press' – described by US media as 'a tough US global military strategy aimed at promoting internal Russian reforms and "dissolution or at least shrinkage" of the Soviet empire.'

* * *

> The arms race that the United States in the Reagan era forced upon the Soviet Union reached its desired objective: that the Soviet Union armed itself to death. The consequent economic burden for the USSR led to serious social dislocations in the country, which meant that the leading power of the socialist camp could hardly do justice to its domestic and foreign policy responsibilities.
>
> – Margot Honecker, Minister of Education 1963–89, German Democratic Republic, 2015

The Soviet Union had long stuck to a system of 'strategic parity' of nuclear weapons development, sparing no effort to keep up with (but not surpass) the United States. As long as it had the ability to retaliate against any US-initiated nuclear strike, it could more or less guarantee that such a strike wouldn't take place – such is the brutal but compelling logic of 'mutually assured destruction'.

At the core of Reagan's full-court press was a strategy to bankrupt the Soviet Union by vastly increasing military expenditure, forcing the USSR to follow suit. Sam Marcy observed in 1987 that 'the Reagan administration went all out and spent more than $2 trillion to overwhelm the USSR. Previous agreements on nuclear treaties, which seemed to have stabilized the situation, were undermined by the Reagan administration.'

Capitalism has a built-in advantage over socialism in areas of production that do not directly benefit people. In a capitalist economy, an arms race creates demand (for high-tech weaponry), which stimulates investment, which creates profit, which keeps the ruling (capitalist) class happy, which in turn keeps its governments stable. In a socialist economy – oriented specifically to meeting people's needs rather than generating profit for a small minority – an increased focus on military development requires divestment of resources from other areas of production – 'diverting material and human resources from the civilian to the military economy, to meet the challenge of Western military pressure', as Stephen Gowans (2012) put it. Given slowed economic growth, plus ongoing problems with food production, housing provision and light manufacturing, the arms race caused genuine difficulties for the USSR. These served to make the ruling (working) class less happy and the domestic political situation less stable.

Although Western propaganda predictably portrayed the Soviet Union as a hostile, aggressive power, the Soviet government was in fact desperate to put an end to the arms race and to agree to a stable *detente*. The USSR unilaterally committed to a no-first-strike policy, and put forward a range of disarmament proposals, including a two-thirds reduction of medium-range weapons by both the USSR and NATO.

Soviet political scientist Boris Ponomarev summed up the USSR's attitude concisely,

> The arms race has been imposed on the Soviet Union entirely by the US and other NATO countries. The US has taken the initiative all along in developing and perfecting nuclear weapons and their delivery vehicles ever since the advent of the atom bomb. Each time the USSR was forced to respond to the challenge to strengthen its own defences, to protect the countries of the socialist community and to keep its armed forces adequately equipped with up-to-date weaponry. But the Soviet Union has been and remains the most consistent advocate of the limitation of the arms race, a champion of disarmament under effective international control. Since the end of World War II the USSR has tabled dozens of proposals in this area. . . . The arms race being whipped up by imperialism has already produced giant arsenals of lethal weapons of unprecedented destructive capacity and has devoured colossal resources that could otherwise have been used for the benefit of mankind.

Contrast this with the leading representative of the US ruling class,

Ronald Reagan, arguing in March 1983 for a ramping up of US nuclear arms production and for a permanent end to *detente*,

> In your discussions of the nuclear freeze proposals, I urge you to beware the temptation of pride – the temptation of blithely declaring yourselves above it all and label both sides equally at fault, to ignore the facts of history and the aggressive impulses of an evil empire, to simply call the arms race a giant misunderstanding and thereby remove yourself from the struggle between right and wrong and good and evil. . . . The reality is that we must find peace through strength. (Clines 1983)

Showing off the depth of his ideologically-driven idiocy, he added: 'I would rather see my little girls die now, still believing in God, than have them grow up under communism and one day die no longer believing in God.'

The escalation in rhetoric was accompanied by an escalation in economic warfare and geostrategic manoeuvring. Keeran and Kenny (2004) point out that the US aimed to

> deny high technology to the Soviet Union and reduce European imports of Soviet gas and oil. By 1983, American high-tech exports to the Soviet Union were valued at only $39 million compared to $219 million in 1975. This economic warfare did not stop with denying the Soviets access to high-tech; the US also sabotaged the goods the Soviets did receive.

Meanwhile, realizing that the Soviets were heavily dependent on oil exports to generate hard currency with which they could pay for the imports they needed from the West (particularly grain and high-tech products), the United States organized for its client states in the Persian Gulf to increase oil production, thereby reducing the price of oil on the world market.

The defining moment of the arms race was Reagan's announcement of the Strategic Defence Initiative (SDI) – 'Star Wars', an anti-ballistic missile system designed to prevent the possibility of nuclear missile attacks against the United States. Although not discussed in such blunt terms, its military objective was to disrupt the system of mutually assured destruction and strategic parity, allowing the US to freely engage in nuclear blackmail. An additional aim was to entice the USSR into developing a rival system, thereby further damaging the Soviet economy. In the end, Star Wars was abandoned – having had around $100 billion thrown at it. The United States did not succeed in building a nuclear missile defence system on anywhere near the scale it had planned, but it did succeed in inspiring another round of frantic investment in military R&D in the USSR.

* * *

In the late 1970s and early 1980s, the global situation would have appeared to the Soviet leaders as being quite positive, with the defeat of US imperialism in Vietnam, the first socialist revolution in the Caribbean (in Grenada), the victory of the revolutionary national liberation movements in Mozambique, Angola, Guinea-Bissau and Zimbabwe, the Sandinista revolution in Nicaragua, along with revolutionary experiments in Ethiopia and Afghanistan. Ponomarev wrote breathlessly of these developments in 1983:

> Revolutionary processes are now at work in many developing countries. The national democratic revolution in Afghanistan under the leadership of the People's Democratic Party has enabled the people of that country to topple the former reactionary anti-popular regime and to embark on the path of progressive socio-economic development. The victorious revolution in Ethiopia, the revolutionary liberation of the peoples of Angola, Mozambique and other former colonies of Portugal, the ending of the racialist regime and the gaining of independence by the people of

> Zimbabwe gave an inspiring impetus to the progressive forces of Africa. The victory of the popular revolution in Nicaragua, the rising tide of liberation struggles in Central America and the Caribbean have signified an expansion of the zone of freedom in the Western hemisphere. The peoples of South Yemen, the People's Republic of the Congo and of some other countries are following the path of socialist development.

By this time, however, the Western powers were engaged in a massive 'rollback' programme, supporting rebellions against progressive governments in Angola, Afghanistan, Nicaragua, Ethiopia, Mozambique, Cambodia and South Yemen. Vijay Prashad (2014) writes that the CIA and the Pentagon 'abandoned the idea of the mere "containment" of communism in favour of using military force to push back against its exertions – even when these were met with massive popular support'. All the states under attack had an urgent need for military and civilian aid, which the Soviet Union had little choice but to provide. In 1983 the United States took advantage of the chaotic situation in Grenada's ruling New Jewel Movement to overturn the Grenadian Revolution by means of military invasion. Meanwhile, Vietnam and Cuba continued to be very reliant on Soviet generosity. The USSR was becoming over-extended, spending up to 30 per cent of its GDP on arms and sponsoring its allies to the tune of tens of billions of dollars each year. This spending may well have been unavoidable – it is hardly reasonable to deny the state of siege imposed on the socialist world by the capitalist world – but it inevitably had an adverse impact on *domestic living conditions.*

* * *

Combined with the military escalation, the US also pursued a 'peaceful evolution' strategy, stepping up its support for the dissident movement in the USSR and for assorted 'pro-democracy' (pro-capitalist) movements in Eastern/Central Europe. *Radio Free Europe* and *Radio Liberty* spearheaded a round of intense ideological warfare, fomenting nationalism, opposing Soviet foreign policy, and giving a platform to dissidents and free-market fundamentalists.

Speaking in 1979, Andropov pointed towards the pro-Western orientation of, and imperialist support for, the dissident movement:

> A few individuals have divorced themselves from Soviet society and engage in anti-Soviet activity, violate the law, supply the west with slanderous information, circulate false rumours, and attempt to provoke various antisocial incidents. These renegades have not and cannot have any support within the country. This is precisely why they do not dare to come out openly at a factory, on a collective farm or in an office. They would have to take to their heels from there, figuratively speaking. The existence of the so-called 'dissidents' has been made possible exclusively by the fact that the enemies of socialism have geared the western press, diplomatic, as well as intelligence and other special services to work in this field. It is no longer a secret to anyone that 'dissidence' has become a profession of its own kind, which is generously rewarded with foreign currency and other sops that differ but little, in effect, from what the imperialist special services pay to their agents.

China expert David Shambaugh points out that the concept of 'peaceful evolution' figures prominently in the Chinese Communist Party's post-mortem on European socialism:

> Chinese analysts, and the CCP itself, have been obsessed with this subject and have alleged a US strategy for years – dating back to John Foster Dulles's first use of the term in the 1950s. Peaceful evolution strategies are said to employ a variety of what today would be described as 'soft power' tools: shortwave radio broadcasts, the promotion of human rights and democracy, economic aid, support for nongovernmental organizations

> and autonomous trade unions, spreading the ideology of capitalism and freedom, supporting underground activists, infiltrating Western media publications into closed countries, academic and cultural exchanges, and so on. Peaceful evolution was said to be the 'soft twin' of 'hard containment'.

Probably the most important element of the 'full-court press', however, was US support for the Mujahedin uprising in Afghanistan, which led to manifold economic and political difficulties in the Soviet Union.

* * *

Making up a considerable part of the Soviet Union's southern border, Afghanistan had always been important to the USSR. The first treaty of friendship between the two countries was signed in 1921 (indeed it was one of the first agreements signed between the Soviet Union and *any* country). The crucial nature of Soviet–Afghan relations is illustrated by the fact that, in his 1924 book *Foundations of Leninism* (a key text seeking to summarize Marxism-Leninism in a way that could be easily digested by the Soviet masses), Stalin discusses the ideological basis of Soviet support for Afghanistan in its struggle against British domination,

> The revolutionary character of a national movement under the conditions of imperialist oppression does not necessarily presuppose the existence of proletarian elements in the movement, the existence of a revolutionary or a republican programme of the movement, the existence of a democratic basis of the movement. The struggle that the Emir of Afghanistan is waging for the independence of Afghanistan is objectively a revolutionary struggle, despite the monarchist views of the Emir and his associates, for it weakens, disintegrates and undermines imperialism.

Good relations between the two countries survived the entire period of existence of the USSR. Although there were some ups and downs in the relationship – largely related to whether the Afghan administration under the extended rule of King Zahir Shah (lasting from 1933 through 1973) was leaning more towards the US or the USSR at any given moment – Afghanistan was generally considered a friendly neighbour, and its leaders had a vision of independence and national modernization that the Soviet Union supported.

From the mid-1950s onwards, Afghanistan was the beneficiary of significant aid, investment and preferential loans from the USSR. Nikita Khrushchev and Nikolai Bulganin announced the first major development loan – worth $100 million – on visiting Kabul in 1955. In the ensuing decades, hospitals, schools, roads, irrigation systems, plumbing systems, factories, power stations and more were built (and sometimes operated) with Soviet assistance. Tens of thousands of Afghans were educated in Soviet universities.

The first Afghan communist organizations were set up in the mid-1960s: *Eternal Flame*, which was strongly aligned with China, and the People's Democratic Party of Afghanistan (PDPA), which was closer to the Soviet Union. The PDPA split soon after its formation into two rival factions – the Khalq ('masses') and the Parcham ('banner') – whose murderous feud would be one of the defining problems of Afghan politics for the ensuing two decades.

Faced with increasingly harsh repression by the state forces headed by President Mohammed Daoud (whom the PDPA had helped to seize power in 1973), the PDPA leadership made the decision to leverage its significant support base in the army to take power, in what became known as the Saur (April) Revolution. The Presidential Palace in Kabul was stormed on April 28, 1978, Daoud and his guards were killed, and the Democratic Republic of Afghanistan (DRA) was proclaimed, with veteran communists Nur Mohammad Taraki and Babrak Karmal as its president and vice president.

The proclaimed objective of the new government was to break the centuries-old grip of feudalism and to establish Afghanistan as a progressive, modern country – a tall order for a country that faced infant mortality levels of 269 per thousand, an average life expectancy of 35, a literacy rate below 10 per cent and a primary school attendance rate of 17 per cent. *Half the population* suffered from tuberculosis and *one-quarter* from malaria. Women in the villages faced the suffocation of patriarchy, were forced to wear the chadri (veil) and were denied access to education. Forced marriage, child marriage and bride-price were pervasive in the countryside.

The essence of the PDPA's programme reflected the urgent need to improve conditions in the countryside – land to the peasants, food for the hungry, free education for all. A PDPA militant reflected later,

> We knew that the mullahs in the villages would scheme against us, so we issued our decrees swiftly so that the masses could see where their real interests lay . . . For the first time in Afghanistan's history women were to be given the right to education . . . We told them that they owned their bodies, they could marry whom they liked, they shouldn't have to live shut up in houses like pets. (Quoted in Braithwaite 2011)

The PDPA government introduced laws cancelling all debt for poor peasants (thereby benefiting two-thirds of the population) and initiating land reform. It made a clear commitment to gender equality, setting up public education for girls and abolishing bride-price, arranged marriage and child marriage. Michael Parenti (2001) writes,

> The Taraki government proceeded to legalize labour unions, and set up a minimum wage, a progressive income tax, a literacy campaign, and programmes that gave ordinary people greater access to health care, housing, and public sanitation. Fledgling peasant cooperatives were started and price reductions on some key foods were imposed. . . . The

> Taraki government moved to eradicate the cultivation of opium poppy. Until then Afghanistan had been producing more than 70 per cent of the opium needed for the world's heroin supply. The government also abolished all debts owed by farmers, and began developing a major land reform programme.

These changes were not to everybody's taste. In the capital, Kabul, the PDPA's initiatives won widespread support. The landlords in the countryside, however, were able to tap into a deep-rooted social conservatism in order to stoke up opposition to the government. Afghan central governments have always had limited control over the villages and tribes, and the more stable governments have enjoyed an uneasy accommodation with the countryside that consists of leaving it to its own devices. For a socialist government determined to break the back of feudalism, however, this was not an acceptable option.

Land reform, debt cancellation and gender equality should have been popular among the masses of poor peasants, but the landowners and mullahs had better access to these people and were able to convince many of them that the PDPA's programme was a ruthless attack on Islam by godless urban communists.

Writing just a few months after the PDPA's capture of power, the British Marxist Fred Halliday (1978) described the early beginnings of the organized opposition to the DRA:

> The forces of counter-revolution have, after initial hesitations, begun to reassemble. Most of the royal family itself is now either dead or complacently exiled, and is unlikely to lead a counter-revolution; but other forces that benefited from the old order are active. These include landowners, tribal chiefs, upper civil servants and mullahs, and there are reports of thousands fleeing to Pakistan where they have predictably appealed for help to Saudi Arabia and Iran.... Taraki has made a point of inviting tribal delegations led by their khans to come to Kabul and meet

> him – in the historic traditions of Afghan rulers – and has repeatedly stressed the DRA's respect for Islam. Nevertheless, the dangers of counter-revolutionary action, given the nature of Afghan society, the weakness of the PDPA and the ferocity of the DRA's enemies, must be substantial.

He added, with remarkable prescience, 'It is evident that a peasantry plagued by tribalism and religious mystification can, under certain circumstances, be temporarily mobilized to fight a new urban-based revolutionary regime. The United States, China, Iran and Pakistan could all exploit the DRA's difficulties.' The US and Pakistan immediately started to assist anti-PDPA groups. As Halliday predicted, it was not difficult to find Afghans willing to take up arms against the government, particularly when these (increasingly sophisticated) arms were accompanied by a steady income paid for by Pakistan and Saudi Arabia. The CIA and ISI (Pakistan's Inter-Services Intelligence) coordinated to launch – as Parenti notes – 'a large scale intervention into Afghanistan on the side of the ousted feudal lords, reactionary tribal chieftains, mullahs, and opium traffickers'.

Zbigniew Brzezinski, then National Security Advisor to US president Jimmy Carter, later admitted that the operation against the Afghan government started well before the arrival of the Soviet army:

> According to the official version of history, CIA aid to the Mujaheddin began during 1980, that is to say, after the Soviet army invaded Afghanistan on December 24, 1979. But the reality, closely guarded until now, is completely otherwise: Indeed, it was July 3, 1979 that President Carter signed the first directive for secret aid to the opponents of the pro-Soviet regime in Kabul. (Gibbs 2000)

Faced with major outbreaks of resistance to government authority – most prominently the Herat uprising of March 1979 – the PDPA was forced to defend itself through heavy repression against the insurgents. Rodric Braithwaite estimates that 'by midsummer 1979 the government controlled perhaps no more than half the country'. To make matters worse, the longstanding split within the PDPA between the Khalq (led by President Taraki and his minister of national defence, Hafizullah Amin) and the Parcham (led by Vice President Karmal) had deteriorated again after a period of tense unity. The leading Parchamites were dispatched as ambassadors to various far-flung countries, and many lower-ranking ones were shot.

Throughout 1979, the Afghan government made repeated requests to the Soviet Union to intervene militarily to save the Saur Revolution from a reactionary, US-backed uprising. Fearing a final collapse of their strategy of *detente* with the West – not to mention the possibility of upsetting their allies in the developing countries ('all the nonaligned countries will be against us', predicted Soviet foreign minister Andrei Gromyko) – the Soviet leadership was not at all keen to get involved beyond providing weaponry, advice and economic support to the PDPA.

The turning point came when violent disagreements and recriminations, no doubt fuelled in part by the increasingly worrying and unstable situation in the country as a whole, led to an intense power struggle between the most prominent Khalq leaders, Taraki and Amin. Amin gained the upper hand, removing Taraki from power and ordering his death on September 14, 1979. This turn of events caused the Soviets to reassess their strategy. They had considered Taraki more trustworthy than Amin and were justifiably concerned that the murderous infighting within the PDPA was jeopardizing the efforts to defeat the insurgency. 'Step by step, with great reluctance, strongly suspecting that it would be a mistake,' Braithwaite writes, 'the Russians slithered towards a military intervention because they could not think of a better alternative.'

The first Russian troops crossed the border into Afghanistan on December 25, 1979. The scope of their mission was limited: help their contacts in the PDPA to overthrow Amin and establish the Parcham leader Babrak Karmal as head of state; end the feuding in the PDPA; help the Afghan Army gain the upper hand against the uprising; and come home soon. There was absolutely no question of wanting to colonize or occupy Afghanistan.

More than a little hypocritically, the US administration led a campaign of global outrage against the Soviet intervention, claiming it was a violation of international law and an example of imperialism. Sanctions against the Soviet Union were hurriedly put in place, as the Western powers boycotted the 1980 Moscow Olympics. More importantly,

> The Soviet intervention was a golden opportunity for the CIA to transform the tribal resistance into a holy war, an Islamic jihad to expel the godless communists from Afghanistan. Over the years the United States and Saudi Arabia expended about $40 billion on the war in Afghanistan. The CIA and its allies recruited, supplied, and trained almost 100,000 radical Mujahedin from forty Muslim countries including Pakistan, Saudi Arabia, Iran, Algeria, and Afghanistan itself. Among those who answered the call was Saudi-born millionaire right-winger Osama bin Laden and his cohorts. (Parenti 2001)

In spite of their public displays of horror, the evidence indicates that the US was more than happy to see the Soviet Union intervene military in Afghanistan. Brzezinski was candid on this point:

> We didn't push the Russians to intervene, but we knowingly increased the probability that they would. . . . That secret operation [support for the Mujahedin from mid-1979] was an excellent idea. It had the effect of drawing the Russians into the Afghan trap and you want me to regret it? The day that the Soviets officially crossed the border, I wrote to President Carter, essentially: 'We now have the opportunity of giving to the USSR

> its Vietnam war.' Indeed, for almost 10 years, Moscow had to carry on a war that was unsustainable for the regime, a conflict that bought about the demoralization and finally the breakup of the Soviet empire. (Interview published in Gibbs 2000)

Vast quantities of money and weapons were channelled to the Afghan resistance via Pakistani military intelligence, who established training camps on the Afghan border, designed supply routes, and worked feverishly (albeit largely fruitlessly) to establish some unity between the seven major Islamist resistance groups.

For the Soviets, the intervention turned out to be much more difficult than they had imagined. Their Afghan allies were divided and often demoralized; meanwhile their enemies were armed with sophisticated weaponry, had significant support among the local population, were fuelled by a vehement hatred of the infidel communist invaders, and were able to leverage Afghanistan's mountainous territory to their advantage. Furthermore, the Red Army was not trained for a counter-insurgency war. The last major war it had fought was the Second World War. The war it was trained to fight was a defensive operation against a large-scale NATO land invasion and aerial bombardment. Fighting mujahids in mountain hideouts was a long way outside the Soviet generals' comfort zone.

Odd Arne Westad (2005) writes that

> From 1981 onwards the war turned into a bloody stalemate, in which more than one million Afghans died and at least 25,000 Soviets. In spite of well-planned efforts, the Red Army simply could not control the areas that were within their operational zones – they advanced into rebel strongholds, kept them occupied for weeks or months, and then had to withdraw as the Mujahedin concentrated its forces or, more often, because its opponents attacked elsewhere.

While there were undoubtedly atrocities on both sides, the Soviets as a whole acted honourably, conceiving of their mission as an internationalist duty to aid a fraternal state that was being subjected to a US-sponsored war of regime change. In the areas that they controlled, they built schools, wells, irrigation systems and power stations, and helped the local population to live something along the lines of a normal life. British journalist Jonathan Steele (2003), an opponent of the Soviet intervention, writes, 'What I saw in 1981, and on three other visits to several cities over the 14 years that the PDPA was in charge, convinced me that it was a much less bad option than the regime on offer from the western-supported Mujahedin.' Braithwaite concurs:

> When I visited Afghanistan in September 2008 . . . I was told by almost every Afghan I met that things were better under the Russians. . . . The Russians, I was told, had built the elements of industry, whereas now most of the aid money simply ended up in the wrong pockets in the wrong countries. In the Russian time everyone had had work; now things were getting steadily worse. The last Communist president, Najibullah, had been one of the best of Afghanistan's recent rulers: more popular than Daoud, the equal of Zahir Shah. Video recordings of Najibullah's speeches were being sold round Kabul, with their warnings – which turned out to be true – that there would be civil war if he were overthrown.

The Red Army did not lose any of its major battles in Afghanistan; it won control of hundreds of towns, villages and roads, only to lose them again when its focus moved elsewhere. The United States deployed increasingly sophisticated weaponry to the rebel groups at just the right rate so as to prevent the Soviet Union from either winning or withdrawing. Taking over as president in 1981, Reagan majorly stepped up US support for the Mujahedin, and from 1985 the weapons deliveries were increased by a factor of ten and came to include the famous FIM-92 Stinger infrared homing surface-to-air missiles.

After several rounds of negotiations and failed attempts to get assurances from Pakistan and the United States that they would not continue to pursue regime change if the Red Army left, the Soviet Union began a phased withdrawal on May 15, 1988. It had not been defeated as such, but it had manifestly failed in the objective of cementing PDPA rule and suppressing the reactionary uprising. Meanwhile, it had expended vast economic, military and human resources. Thousands of young lives were lost. Soviet diplomatic clout had reached its nadir. As the Soviets had themselves predicted, the intervention in Afghanistan weakened their position among the developing nations: 'The Soviet entry into Afghanistan divided the non-aligned states. It weakened their bloc in the UN, where eighteen countries (led by Algeria, India, and Iraq) refused to go along with the US resolution asking for the Soviet withdrawal', as pointed out by Prashad (2014). Furthermore, the tens of thousands who came home badly injured from Afghanistan mostly found that they were not well cared for in terms of housing, pensions and psychological support; their fallen comrades were not, for the most part, given a status befitting their internationalist mission. This correlated with the expanding anti-communism and nihilism of the Gorbachev era.

Beyond the direct economic impact, the Afghanistan war served to further undermine Soviet self-confidence and the popular legitimacy of its government. As Westad (2005) summarized the situation,

> To the great majority of Soviets the involvement in Afghanistan had become a byword for an unloved and increasingly superfluous role that their government played in the Third World. To them, withdrawing from Kabul therefore meant the end of a failed intervention. By 1989 the common pride in the Soviet global role that had existed only a few years before was no longer there. It had been replaced not only by a lack of faith in the Soviet system, but also by a conviction that its leaders squandered their resources abroad while people at home lived in poverty. . . . Since

> a substantial part of the CPSU regime's overall legitimacy was based on its superpower role abroad, the failure in Afghanistan became a deadly challenge to the key concepts of its foreign policy: Soviet military power and the global advance of socialism.

Some US hawks – and indeed some Mujahedin leaders – claimed that it was the failure in Afghanistan that brought about the end of the Soviet Union. Burhanuddin Rabbani, a prominent Mujahedin leader who would go on to become President of the Islamic State of Afghanistan from 1992 to 1996, proclaimed,

> We forced the communists out of our country, we can force all invaders out of holy Afghanistan . . . Had it not been for the jihad, the whole world would still be in the communist grip. The Berlin Wall fell because of the wounds which we inflicted on the Soviet Union, and the inspiration we gave all oppressed people. We broke the Soviet Union up into fifteen parts. We liberated people from communism. Jihad led to a free world. We saved the world because communism met its grave here in Afghanistan! (Quoted in Braithwaite 2011)

The reality is, as ever, more complex. The Afghan war was just one of several factors in the Soviet collapse; after all, the US sustained a comprehensive and shameful defeat in Vietnam, but this did not come close to bringing about its collapse as a political entity. The economic decline, the leadership's attack on Soviet ideology and history, the ongoing process of destabilization and disinformation – these were all more important contributors to the disintegration of the USSR. But unquestionably the Afghan debacle played its part.

CHAPTER 5

Perestroika and Glasnost

> The basic cause of the dissolution of the Soviet Union may be identified as the long-term ideological chaos that prevailed in the USSR. Acting as a key driver of events were long-term mistakes in organizational policy, while the primary factor that dealt the direct, fatal blow was political betrayal, through the implementation of 'perestroika and new thinking'.
>
> – Cheng Enfu and Liu Zixu (2017)

After a decade of economic stagnation, declining popular confidence and escalating military confrontation with the West – and with three CPSU general secretaries in three years having died on the job (Brezhnev, Andropov and Chernenko) – there was an obvious need to breathe some new life into Soviet politics. Andropov understood this better than most; during his brief tenure, he encouraged younger members of the Party's Central Committee to help modernize Soviet socialism. Mikhail Gorbachev, elected by the Politburo as General Secretary after the death of Chernenko in March 1985, was part of this 'new generation'. He was chosen, Braithwaite (2011) writes, 'because he was young, energetic, imaginative, and – [the Central Committee] believed – orthodox'.

The early signs were promising: Gorbachev promoted a vision of enhancing socialist democracy and modernizing the economy whilst maintaining social ownership of the means of production and preserving the political power of the working class. Keeran and Kenny (2004) write:

> Gorbachev advocated the elimination of wage levelling. In a swipe at the illegal parts of the second economy and corruption, he called for a struggle against 'unearned incomes' and all 'phenomena that are alien to the socialist way of life'. In foreign policy, Gorbachev reaffirmed such traditional Soviet positions as the support of national liberation, peaceful coexistence, and cooperation with the West on 'principles of equality'. He gave special emphasis to ending the arms race and freezing nuclear arsenals.
>
> In politics, Gorbachev proposed 'strengthening' and 'heightening' the leading role of the Party, a 'strict observance of the Leninist style of work' and the elimination of 'false idealization' and formalism in Party meetings. Gorbachev spoke of the need for glasnost, or 'greater openness and publicity' about the work of the Party, state and other public organizations.

Gorbachev talked of the need for *perestroika* – restructuring. This term, never very well defined, ultimately became a byword for the systematic destruction of Soviet socialism. However, this is presumably not how it was conceived of, and certainly not how it was presented to the Soviet people. Yegor Ligachev, Gorbachev's second-in-command from 1985 to 1988, was a keen supporter of perestroika as it was presented in its early years (he later earned the epithet 'leading hardliner' from the Western press after he fell out with Gorbachev). In his memoirs, he boils down his understanding of the principal aims of perestroika:

> 1. Making some limited use of market mechanisms to increase production and innovation, within the context of the planned economy.
> 2. Renewing economic infrastructure.
> 3. Investing heavily in technology and science.

4. Increasing popular participation in existing democratic systems.
5. Pushing hard for multilateral nuclear disarmament.

These objectives sounded, and sound, sensible enough. Unfortunately, they bear little relation to what actually took place in the name of perestroika. Gorbachev's reforms didn't strengthen socialism; rather, they laid the grounds for economic ruin and for the hollowing out of the Communist Party, which was transformed into little more than a training ground for budding manager-capitalists to gain control of assets that would later make them enormously rich.

With the economy spiralling out of control and the Party reduced to a shadow of its former self, alternative – explicitly nationalist and anti-communist – centres of power arose to fill the political vacuum. With the support of a nascent capitalist class and the global mass media (not to mention Western governments and intelligence agencies), these organizations gained sufficient strength that they were able to force through the disintegration of the Soviet Union, the banning of the Communist Party, the dismantling of socialism, and the introduction of the harshest possible neoliberal capitalist 'shock therapy'. Such was the harvest of perestroika.

* * *

Although Gorbachev and his team would later claim they had inherited a society in crisis, this was not actually the case. There was no serious public unrest in 1985. In spite of assorted economic problems and a degree of popular dissatisfaction (hardly unusual in any society), there was not any serious trouble, and very few people would have imagined that within a few years Soviet socialism would no longer exist. Polls consistently indicated that people were broadly content with the status quo. The political system was widely accepted. The economy was growing, albeit slowly. Everybody had their basic needs met in terms of food, shelter, heating, clothing and healthcare. Education and cultural facilities were world class. The social welfare system was unparalleled outside the socialist world. The streets were safe, and people had the opportunity to live interesting, fulfilling, productive lives. Whilst most people recognized that living standards were higher in the US and parts of Europe, they also understood that the socialist system offered them a level of personal safety, community spirit and educational/cultural opportunity that wouldn't be available to them in the West.

As the Western media became very fond of pointing out (and exaggerating), there were some shortages of consumer goods, leading to queues in shops. While this indicates inefficiencies in distribution (and wider economic problems), it does not testify to dire poverty or social collapse. As Samir Amin (2016) puts it,

> It is obvious that if prices rise massively, there are no more queues, but the seemingly vanished poverty is still there for those who no longer have access to consumer goods. The shops in Mexico and Egypt are packed with goods, and there are no lines in front of the butchers' shops, but meat consumption per head is a third of what it was in Eastern Europe.

The Soviet Union's allies were facing difficult times in Afghanistan, Nicaragua and Ethiopia, but were in the ascendancy in southern Africa – particularly Angola. Vietnam's economic situation started to improve rapidly after its adoption of *Doi Moi* reforms in 1986, and therefore its reliance on Soviet aid was reduced. Cuba and the Democratic People's Republic of Korea were doing reasonably well. After a very painful quarter of a century, there finally seemed to be a possibility of overcoming the Sino-Soviet split (ties were finally normalized in 1989 – by which time, sadly, the USSR was in its death throes). And although the Reagan administration had stepped up US economic, military and political operations against the Soviet Union, the latter was holding its own.

In short, the USSR in the mid-1980s was not a society on the verge of collapse.

* * *

In the field of economics, the major objective of perestroika was – as Sam Marcy (1990) writes – to 'modernize and streamline the Soviet economy through the introduction of new management techniques and technology in use elsewhere in the world, particularly in the highly developed imperialist countries'. The vision was, within 15 years, 'to create an economic potential approximately equal in scale to that accumulated throughout all the previous years of Soviet government and to almost double national income and industrial output. Productivity of labour is to go up by 130–150 per cent. . . . The implementation of the programme will . . . raise the Soviet people's standard of living to a qualitatively new level.'

The two major strategic themes put forward in order to reach these goals were: first, the extension of market relations within the overall context of public ownership, in order to boost innovation and productivity; second, an attempt to 'democratize planning' by pulling the plug on the entire central planning system. The former theme was not entirely without merit – it has worked well in China and Vietnam, for example. Dismantling the planning system, on the other hand, created unmitigated havoc, as a result of which the USSR, in 1990, experienced negative growth for the first time in its history.

Gorbachev's initial steps in the economy were interesting but inept. The first big reform was an anti-alcohol campaign with partial prohibition announced in May 1985. Intended to help alleviate the major problems the Soviet Union was experiencing in terms of public health and labour productivity (particularly absenteeism), the reform consisted of a price hike for all alcoholic drinks, reduced production of vodka and wine, an increase in the minimum drinking age (to 21), stiff penalties on drunken behaviour, the banning of alcohol consumption in the workplace, and various regulations in relation to the sale of alcohol. Well-intentioned as the campaign may have been, it was a near-complete failure and had damaging side effects. Kotz and Weir (1997) point out that

> While a slight increase in sobriety may have resulted, this campaign, like the American experiment with Prohibition after World War I, had unforeseen harmful consequences. Illegal private production arose to meet the unsatisfied demand. Private distillers stripped the retail stores of sugar, causing severe shortages. And an estimated 20 billion roubles in tax revenues were lost on alcohol sales during 1986–88.

The loss in income was a fairly serious blow to an already troubled economy that derived a substantial portion of its fiscal revenue from the state monopoly on alcohol. Furthermore, the sharp growth in production of illicit moonshine meant that there was no long-term improvement in labour productivity or public health. It also served to extend the underground economy, thereby contributing to the growth of a nascent bourgeoisie with an interest in expanding its market and legitimizing its activities. Gorbachev himself would later acknowledge that 'the anti-alcohol campaign and how it was implemented was a mistake in the long run' ('Booze booboo: Gorbachev admits', 2015).

The Politburo went on to introduce a package of economic reforms that bore some resemblance to the Kosygin–Liberman reforms. The centrepiece was a proposal to allow state production enterprises to determine their own output levels, on the basis that the enterprises had more insight into their capacity, resources and circumstances than the central planners did. Gosplan, the central planning agency, was to withdraw from micromanaging enterprises and switch to long-term goal-setting. Local soviets were to be given a bigger role in management and oversight, and workers were to be given greater decision-making power.

The reform was flawed in a number of respects and had negative repercussions that would undermine the entire economic system. Worse, the leadership did not back out of the reform once it was clear that it was not working; it was sudden and risky, imposed by the top-level state machinery without suitable mechanisms for feedback and improvement. There was certainly no 'crossing the river by feeling the stones'; it was more like taking a big leap into the middle of the river and hoping for the best. It is perhaps useful to compare this approach with the methodology used in China's economic reforms, for example the *household responsibility system*, a decentralized method of agricultural production that was tried out at the level of a single village (illegally, in fact) and which was sufficiently successful in boosting agricultural output that it was gradually rolled out at regional and national level over the course of a few years. Of this system, Justin Yifu Lin (2011) writes,

> The household responsibility system was not designed by any leader – it was a product of villagers in Xiaogang village in Fengyang county, Anhui province. Driven by bad weather and low production in 1978, they took responsibility for their own gains and losses, with a proviso that if any of them were to go to jail for secretly embarking on this illegal system, the others would take care of their children. Seeing the incredible results, the Central Rural Work Conference at the end of 1979 decided that the poorest residents in rural areas would be allowed to engage in this system. At the end of 1980, 14% of the production teams around the country followed the system. . . . All production teams under the household responsibility system had remarkable results that year. So in 1981 the government started to promote the system across the country.

By the end of the year, 45% of production teams were in the system, in 1982, 80%, and in 1984, 99%.

The most immediately visible result of Gorbachev's reform package was to create shortages of certain goods. Enterprises were now able to determine their own product mix, but there was no corresponding change in the *market* for those products: prices remained fixed by the state, and therefore most enterprises simply focused on producing those items that had the highest mark-up. Allen Lynch (2012) writes:

> Most Soviet factories simply stopped making low margin consumer items, and massive shortages of everyday items quickly set in (e.g. salt, sugar, matches, cooking oil, washing powder, baby clothes, etc.). By mid-1989, coal miners in Donbass had no soap to wash with after a long day in the mines, a development that triggered massive strikes and a coalition of workers and intellectuals against the Soviet system and Gorbachev himself.

With more direct control over their spending, many of the enterprises chose to pay their workers more. Given endemic labour shortages, increasing wages would have felt like a sensible policy at the level of the individual enterprise, because it was a means of attracting and retaining workers. However, at a broader level, the combination of higher wages, ever-worsening shortages of consumer goods and state-fixed low prices served to create repressed inflation. This in turn led to increased black-market activity and speculation, undermining the overall economy. Furthermore, increased wages tended to mean less resources for investment; the future was sacrificed for the sake of the present. The result was a further decline in innovation and productivity growth. And although all of this was done in the name of 'democratizing' production, the new system allowed enterprise managers to exercise unchecked control over vast resources – a position that many of them leveraged to their advantage in the wild-west asset-stripping days of the early 1990s.

Late in 1987, Gorbachev pushed through a major decrease in state purchases of industrial output, thus forcing the enterprises to sink or swim in the open market, regardless of whether they were anything approximating 'viable' without their guaranteed monopoly. As Keeran and Kenny put it,

> Against the better judgement of Prime Minister Ryzhkov and Ligachev, Yakovlev [Gorbachev's closest adviser] and Gorbachev pushed to shrink the state orders – the guaranteed government purchase of Soviet industrial output at fixed prices – from 100 per cent to a mere 50 per cent of the whole of industry. Reducing state orders to such a degree meant that, in one leap, half of Soviet industry would gain autonomy to buy and sell its output in a new wholesale market – trade between enterprises – with prices set by fluctuations in supply and demand. . . . The Gorbachev plan proved utterly reckless. It plunged the economy into chaos. In 1988, consumer shortages proliferated and, for the first time since World War II, inflation appeared.

With the enterprises thrown into chaos and often struggling to sell their produce in a newly-competitive market, state revenues suffered a sharp reduction. Sitaram Yechury writes that this 'led to a situation where the government had to increasingly resort to budgetary deficits. In 1985 the budget deficit was a modest 18 million roubles which rose to nearly 120 billion by 1989 or 14% of the Soviet Union's GNP' (Prashad 2017). The fiscal deficit drove austerity: 'during Gorbachev's leadership, import of food grains and consumer items fell by the equivalent of 8.5 billion roubles'.

The next major step in Gorbachev's economic reform was the 1988 law on cooperatives, which allowed people to set up their own businesses. British economist Philip Hanson (2014) describes this as 'the most radical of all Gorbachev's economic measures so far. . . . Members of a cooperative could be few or many, and they could employ non-members. A cooperative was therefore capable of being a capitalist partnership, with the members exploiting, in Marxist terms, the labour of non-members.' Strictly speaking these cooperatives were not allowed to employ other people's labour, but in reality this regulation was observed almost exclusively in the breach. Initially, most of the cooperatives were cafés, restaurants, hairdressers and small construction firms – exactly the sort of business that tends to be quite effectively run on a small scale. However, the cooperative movement quickly came to be dominated by 'pocket banks used by their founding enterprises to move funds around discreetly and cooperative banks that were able, when foreign-currency and government debt markets developed, to make large profits from playing very thin financial markets'. Many of the fabulously wealthy Russian gangster-capitalists of the 1990s made their start in 'cooperative' banks in the late 1980s. In addition to paving the way for a new finance-capitalist class, the cooperatives also laid the ground for a lucrative non-productive underground economy: 'Cooperatives providing consumer goods and services, which had to be readily visible to function, soon ran into difficulties from criminal gangs. Protection rackets developed, and the police were unable or unwilling to stop them.'

The increasingly dire situation was not helped by falling oil prices. In 1986, Saudi Arabia increased its oil production by two million barrels a day, causing the world market price to drop precipitously. This had a serious impact on the Soviet economy, which had since the early 1970s relied on high oil prices to cover for weaknesses elsewhere. As long as oil prices were high, there was enough hard currency to import goods and pay debts (a by-product of this is that the Soviet leadership was able to procrastinate on economic reforms, unlike the Chinese leadership which by the late 1970s had very little choice but to fix the economy). Allen Lynch writes, 'Gorbachev was thus forced to undertake the precarious (and as we have seen ill-thought out) programme of structural reform with a radically reduced resource base; the Soviet economy had lost its shock absorber.'

Gorbachev's economic reform package lacked organizational infrastructure. Appropriate institutions might have been able to provide guidance and constrain the new freedom of the enterprises such that reduced investment, imbalanced product mix and repressed inflation were avoided. However, just when institutional supervision was most needed, Gorbachev and his coterie were busy delegitimizing the Communist Party and hollowing out the economic ministries and planning bodies. As Vladislav Zubok (2009) points out, 'instead of relying on the most pragmatic elements of the party and state officialdom in restructuring of the country, Gorbachev tried to build up new political forces and movements while gradually diminishing the power of the party and of centralized state structures'.

The result was chaos. 'The grave economic, financial, and state crisis began only between 1986 and 1988, and it kept growing worse because of Gorbachev's choices and policies.' In place of cautious, measured experiments conducted within a stable political context, Gorbachev set in train a rapid dismantling of the existing system whilst at the same time creating political anarchy. Again, the comparison with China is apposite. As Kotz and Weir point out,

> [In China] there was virtually no privatization – state enterprises were kept under state ownership and control. There was no sudden price liberalization – state enterprises continued to sell at controlled prices. Central planning was retained for the state sector of the economy. Rather than slashing state spending, various levels of government poured funds into improving China's basic economic infrastructure of transportation, communication, and power. Rather than tight monetary policy, ample

credit was provided for expansion and modernization. The state has sought to gradually develop a market economy over a period of decades, and the state has actively guided the process.

Gennady Zyuganov (1997), current leader of the Communist Party of the Russian Federation, is scathing in his assessment of the perestroika package of economic reforms:

> As we know from historical experience, common sense, and scientific analysis, no reform can be implemented successfully without a well-developed programme and precisely defined goals; a team of vigorous and highly intellectual reformers; a strong and effective system for controlling political phenomena; thoroughly developed and carefully considered methods of instituting the reforms; the mobilization of the mass media to explain the meaning, goals, and consequences of the reforms for the state as a whole and for the individual person in particular for the purpose of involving as much of the population as possible in the reform process; and the preservation and development of the structures, relations, functions, methods, and lifestyles that have earned the approval of the people. The reform process in China (PRC) developed along approximately similar lines. But nothing like this was done by Mikhail Gorbachev and his team. Labour collectives, party organizations, economic leaders, and much of the intelligentsia were excluded from participating in the renewal of society. The right to define directions and interpret the meaning of the reorganization processes was appropriated by a small group of top leaders, who were given to superficial improvisation and were unable to organize and direct the reform properly. . . . Instead of the hard work that was urgently needed, they unfolded a parade of political arrogance, demagoguery, and dilettantism, which gradually overwhelmed and paralysed the country.

In 1990, the USSR went into recession for the first time. By 1991, its economy was in free fall.

* * *

> What happened in our country is primarily the result of the debilitation and eventual elimination of the Communist Party's leading role in society, the ejection of the party from major policymaking, its ideological and organizational unravelling, the formation in it of factions, careerists' and national separatists' penetration of the leadership of the party and state as well as the party and power structures of the republics, and the political conversion of the group headed by Gorbachev and their shift to the position of elimination of the Communist Party and the Soviet state.
>
> – Yegor Ligachev

In 1986, Gorbachev and his advisers came up with the concept of *glasnost* ('openness') to encapsulate policies of greater government transparency, wider political discussion and increased popular participation. Corruption and inefficiency would be tackled, and more information would be made publicly available. At first, it sounded fairly innocuous – what reasonable person would object to a deepening of socialist democracy? However, it quickly became a battle cry for an all-out attack on the legitimacy of the Communist Party of the Soviet Union and on the foundations of the Soviet identity. In short, it became a powerful weapon in the hands of social forces hostile to socialism.

It's worth pointing out that Gorbachev never put much meat on the bones of 'democratization'. With hindsight, it's obvious that his use of the term reflected an ideological concession to Western 'liberal' capitalism; that he had come to believe that the Soviet Union should aspire to the political norms defined in Western Europe and the United States. Such thinking neglects a number of factors that should be well understood by any Marxist,

1. 'Free speech' in the advanced capitalist countries is a piece of attractive icing beneath which lies a bitter cake of plutocratic repression. Via its monopolization of the mass media, the ruling class dominates the field of ideas comprehensively. There is a level of debate and criticism, but only of a few individual policies and not of systemic features of capitalism. As Chomsky famously put it, 'The smart way to keep people passive and obedient is to strictly limit the spectrum of acceptable opinion, but allow very lively debate within that spectrum.'
2. The political freedoms available in the West are much constrained owing to the correlation between wealth and power. Ordinary citizens have the right to vote, but their choice is nearly always restricted to two or three pro-capitalist, pro-imperialist parties, between which there is little substantive difference (so rare is the appearance of a meaningfully different option within mainstream politics that, when it happens, it sends the ruling class into a frenzy of confusion). Actual power is monopolized by the wealthy, and challenging it can be extremely dangerous, as is evidenced by the treatment of imprisoned Irish Republicans, or the many longstanding Black, Puerto Rican and indigenous political prisoners in the United States who have spent decades behind bars on account of their struggle for equality and human rights.
3. In a context of ongoing class struggle waged by the working class of a socialist country against its internal enemies (those that want to restore feudalism or capitalism) and its external enemies (the leading capitalist countries that will inevitably work to destabilize a socialist country), a level of political repression is an unhappy necessity. The needs of the few – to get fantastically rich – cannot be allowed to compromise the

> needs of the many to enjoy a dignified, peaceful and fulfilling life.

The Soviet political system was undeniably rife with problems: the alienation and disaffection of young people, excessively centralized decision-making, corruption, arbitrariness by police and officials, insufficient levels of popular participation in the soviets, and more. But these were not problems that could be solved by imitating a Western bourgeois-democratic model that had no cultural and social basis in the USSR. Rather, political reforms should have attempted to build on and improve the existing system.

Difficulties and contradictions notwithstanding, the Soviet Union had built a viable socialist democracy that, in terms of empowering ordinary people, was significantly more inclusive and meaningful than the capitalist democracy of, say, the United States or Britain. For example, Al Szymanski (writing in 1979) describes the way that mass media was used to exchange ideas and inform policy,

> In the Soviet Union, unlike the Western capitalist countries, the major forums for public debate, criticism, and public opinion formation are the mass media, together with specialized journals and conferences. The media are the major forum for opposing views, with *Pravda* and *Izvestia* ranging more freely as social critics than the local weeklies. The Soviet press is full of public debates on a very wide range of issues: literary policy, economic and legal reform, military strategy, the relation between the Party and the military, city planning, crime, pollution, farm problems, the role of the press, art, women's role in the economy, access to higher education, incompetent economic management, bungling bureaucrats, etc.

Szymanski describes 'a few basic assumptions of Soviet society' that were not debated in the press: socialism as a system, communism as a goal, and the leading role of the Communist Party. 'These issues are considered to have been settled once and for all and public discussion of them is considered by the regime to be potentially disruptive of popular rule.' This is consistent with Fidel Castro's famous formula: 'Within the revolution, everything; against the revolution, nothing.' These basic assumptions of socialism can be compared with the basic assumptions of capitalism: the supremacy of private property; profit as the major engine of economic activity; exploitation of labour as the source of profit.

Gorbachev did not have widespread support for his economic reforms within the CPSU. This was partly due to a culture of caution and conservatism within the CPSU, but more importantly because Gorbachev's schemes were not convincing and well thought out. The risk was too great in the eyes of many Party veterans, particularly given the absence of a reasonable plan for gradual reform by carefully managed trial and error and with a clear rollback mechanism.

The initial enthusiasm of 1985–86 had, within a couple of years, given way to a sense of anxiety that the reforms were not solving any problems but were in fact contributing to the increasingly dire status of the economy. Rather than reflecting on whether a different approach was required, Gorbachev instead placed the blame on the Party, which he claimed was opposed to his reforms and eager to see them fail. Writing in May 1988, Sam Marcy observed, 'Perestroika has not in these almost three years been a spectacular success. Gorbachev himself does not claim it has. As a matter of fact, he has often spoken about lack of progress, but blames resistance within the Party, particularly in the lower echelons and the outlying regions of the country.' Keeran and Kenny make a similar observation:

> From the early days Gorbachev saw the CPSU as the main obstacle, and the Party apparatus as his main enemy, not as an instrument to carry

the struggle for reform forward. He had to outmanoeuvre the Party, not struggle within it. He always appealed to intellectuals and the public over the Party's head. Everywhere, his memoirs contain such sentiments as 'Party structures are applying the brakes'.

Glasnost, then, was an attempt to 'unleash the public', where *the public* was defined as people who unambiguously supported perestroika. Continuing support for perestroika was to be found primarily outside the Party leadership, particularly among capitalist restorationists, anti-Soviet nationalists of assorted hue, sections of the intelligentsia, and the new generation of small capitalists and managers that could not wait to get filthy rich.

The first major organizational step towards breaking the CPSU's power was taken at the 19th Party conference in June 1988, which Gorbachev presented with a last-minute surprise proposal that he had been careful not to distribute in advance. The crux of this proposal was to increase the separation of the Party and the state, tilt power towards non-Party structures, stuff these non-Party structures with proponents of the 'new thinking', and create greater executive power for Gorbachev and his allies. A Congress of People's Deputies was to be set up, with two-thirds of its members to be directly elected. This body would then select a legislature of around 500 members (the Supreme Soviet).

The elected chairman of the Supreme Soviet would essentially be an executive president – a post designed by Gorbachev, for Gorbachev. Keeran and Kenny assess that 'the proposal, introduced in the final minutes in a surprise resolution by Gorbachev in the chair, amounted to the overthrow of the Central Committee'. Disoriented by the sudden appearance and radical nature of the proposals, a majority of delegates voted in its favour.

The newly-created organs of power were chaotic, but they were much easier than the older structures for Gorbachev and his team to dominate, since they were largely composed of people that had been encouraged and promoted by Gorbachev and the increasingly anti-communist press. As a result, Gorbachev's team suddenly had a mandate to accelerate the pace of reforms to a dangerous degree. Meanwhile, the new political space provided nutrient-rich soil for assorted right-wing nationalist movements around the country, leading to a bumper yield of insurrection and instability over the course of the ensuing three years.

Gorbachev also moved to change the class composition of the Communist Party. Before the 1988 Party Conference, he said very candidly that only people who supported his programme were eligible to be delegates, 'There must be no more quotas, as we had in the past – so many workers and peasants, so many women, and so forth. The principal political imperative is to elect active supporters of perestroika' (Keller 1988). Cheng Enfu and Liu Zixu observe that, 'in the name of promoting young cadres and of reform, Gorbachev replaced large numbers of party, political and military leaders with anti-CPSU and anti-socialist cadres or cadres with ambivalent positions. This practice laid the foundations, in organizational and cadre selection terms, for the political shift of direction.'

Later in 1988, Gorbachev moved against the more traditionalist (that is: communist) members of the Party leadership. The most senior official, Andrei Gromyko – a key negotiator at Yalta and Potsdam in 1945, foreign minister from 1957 to 1985 and Chairman of the Presidium of the Supreme Soviet from 1985 until 1988 – was removed from the Politburo. Nikolai Baibakov was fired as head of the central planning agency after two decades, in spite of his vast wealth of experience (which included overseeing Russian oil production during the Second World War). Yegor Ligachev, who had become increasingly vocal in his critique of perestroika, was demoted from head of ideology to head of agriculture. As the communists were systematically removed from the Party and state leadership, supporters of 'radical reform' were promoted, including Boris Yeltsin.

Ligachev's role as head of ideology fell to Alexander Yakovlev, Gorbachev's closest political adviser and widely regarded as the 'godfather of glasnost', wielding what Keeran and Kenny describe as 'the most powerful and pernicious influence of anyone on the entire reform process'. We now know that Yakovlev had long since given up on his commitment to Marxism and had his heart set on transforming the Soviet Union into a multi-party parliamentary democracy and market economy along the lines of Canada (where he had spent ten years as Soviet ambassador). Initially he hoped this could be achieved through reforms, but he reveals in his memoirs that, with the reins in his hands, he decided that nothing less than counter-revolution would do.

> In the first years of perestroika most reformers had the illusion that socialism could be improved. The argument was only about the depth of improvement. At some point in 1987, I personally realized that a society based on violence and fear could not be reformed and that we faced a momentous historical task of dismantling an entire social and economic system with all its ideological, economic and political roots. It had become imperative to make profound changes in ideology and overcome its myths and utopias. (Yakovlev 1993)

Given almost complete autonomy in the areas of media and propaganda, Yakovlev went about 'overcoming myths and utopias' by doing everything possible to attack the CPSU and Soviet history. He went so far as to claim that the October Revolution was simply part of Germany's First World War strategy: 'The October Revolution was the action of the German General Staff. Lenin received two million marks in March 1915 for sabotage' (quoted in Shenming 2017).

Dissidents and anti-communists were appointed as editors of newspapers and magazines and were given *carte blanche* to use their publications to openly attack the basic ideas of socialism and the whole nature of the Soviet system. 'Liberal intellectuals were named to run *Ogonyok*, *Sovetskaya Kultura*, *Moscow News*, *Znamya*, and *Novy Mir*', write Kotz and Weir. 'The top political leadership had actually given editors, journalists, writers, and economists freedom to write as they wished, using the mass media as their vehicle.' It is unprecedented in any social system for the ruling class to hand over the state's propaganda apparatus to its class enemy. What Gorbachev, Yakovlev and their coterie did was akin to the British government handing management of the BBC over to the IRA. This was the rotten meat on the bones of Gorbachev's 'freedom of the press'. There was no freedom to criticize perestroika and glasnost, but there was freedom for a full-scale assault on the Party's history and ideology. No accusation went unmade. Zubok explains that

> Gorbachev and his assistants allowed the process of glasnost to go on until it became a whirlwind of revelations that discredited the entire foundation of Soviet foreign policy and the regime itself. . . . Some Moscow-based revisionists began to hold the Soviet Union solely and exclusively responsible for the Cold War. They began to consider the policies of the West to be purely reactive and dictated by the need to fight Stalin's communist aggression and totalitarian threat.

Absurd exaggerations about Stalin's crimes once again became the order of the day; these were in fact stalking horses for attacks on socialist construction and the defence of the Soviet Union against Nazism – the greatest achievements of the Soviet people. 'It is a broad attack against communism, and Stalin is merely a convenient symbol', wrote Sam Marcy in June 1988. This point was powerfully made in a famous letter to the newspaper *Sovetskaya Rossiya* in March 1988 by a Leningrad chemistry teacher by the name of Nina Andreyeva (the letter caused such a stir that Gorbachev used it as the justification for a new round of anti-communist purges). Andreyeva wrote,

> Take the question of the place of JV Stalin in our country's history. It is with his name that the entire obsession with critical attacks is associated, an obsession that, in my opinion, has to do not so much with the historical personality itself as with the whole extremely complex transitional era – an era linked with the unparalleled exploits of an entire generation of Soviet people who today are gradually retiring from active labour, political and public activity. Industrialization, collectivization and the cultural revolution, which brought our country into the ranks of the great world powers, are being forcibly squeezed into the 'personality cult' formula. All these things are being questioned. Things have reached a point at which insistent demands for 'repentance' are being made on 'Stalinists' (and one can assign to their number whoever one wishes). Praise is being lavished on novels and films that lynch the era of tempestuous changes, which is presented as a 'tragedy of peoples'. (Cited in Marcy 1990)

Once the Congress of People's Deputies was established in 1989, its proceedings were televised, another *ad hoc* decision by Gorbachev. 'For thirteen days and nights, the proceedings transfixed two hundred million Soviet viewers', who witnessed well-known personalities arguing persuasively against socialism. For example, on June 2, 1989, Kyrgyz author Chingiz Aitmatov – a close ally of Gorbachev – took the podium to laud the achievements of the 'flourishing, law-abiding societies of Sweden, Austria, Finland, Norway, Holland, Spain and, finally, across the ocean, Canada', adding that 'we've done them a favour by showing them how not to build socialism' (quoted in Hanson 2014). Other speakers attacked the KGB's 'history of crimes'. As Keeran and Kenny put it, they

> demanded Lenin's body be removed from Red Square, denounced the one-party system, and disputed the validity of Marxism. . . . The proceedings of the Congress shook the self-confidence of the CPSU to its foundations. For millions, the Congress undermined the legitimacy of

> the Party, Soviet history, and the whole social order. It also emboldened socialism's opponents. It pushed back the boundaries of the politically thinkable. Managed reform was over. Gorbachev became 'a surfboarder of events'.

Added to all this was the fact that Gorbachev and his allies decided to end restrictions on foreign propaganda, for example putting an end to the jamming of Radio Liberty (Schmemann 1988) – a generously-funded propaganda arm of the CIA, focused on spreading anti-communist lies around the socialist countries of Europe. So Gorbachev's idea of 'improving socialism' was in fact based on bulldozing its structures and legacy.

The attack on the Party went so far that Fidel Castro, in December 1989, at an event commemorating the 2,000-plus Cubans who died in the course of their heroic internationalist duties in Angola, was moved to remark,

> It's impossible to carry out a revolution or conduct a rectification without a strong, disciplined and respected party. It's not possible to carry out such a process by slandering socialism, destroying its values, discrediting the party, demoralizing its vanguard, abandoning its leadership role, eliminating social discipline, and sowing chaos and anarchy everywhere. This may foster a counter-revolution – but not revolutionary change. . . .
>
> It is disgusting to see how many people, even in the Soviet Union itself, are engaged in denying and destroying the history-making feats and extraordinary merits of that heroic people. That is not the way to rectify and overcome the undeniable errors made by a revolution that emerged from tsarist authoritarianism in an enormous, backward, poor country. We shouldn't blame Lenin now for having chosen tsarist Russia as the place for the greatest revolution in history. (Castro et al. 2013)

By 1991, the job of destroying the CPSU was almost entirely

complete. *New York Times* columnist Esther Fein was all too accurate when she opined in July 1991 that 'the Communist Party's decline in power and prestige is perhaps the most critical development in the reform of the political system'. This act of grand-scale political vandalism remains Mikhail Gorbachev's principal endowment to the world.

The outright attack on the CPSU and the undermining of its authority is unique to Gorbachev. His predecessors can be accused of many mistakes, but actively weakening the power of the Communist Party was not one of them. Up until the glasnost period, the Soviet leadership always reiterated the importance of the Party as the leading element in political life. For example Boris Ponomarev, a leading ideologist during the Brezhnev and Andropov periods, wrote just two years before Gorbachev's appointment as General Secretary,

> The leading vanguard position of the Communist Party has been the decisive subjective prerequisite for all the fundamental gains made by the proletariat in the course of the class struggle, for all the victorious socialist revolutions, for all the historic accomplishments by the peoples embarked on the path of socialism and building the new society. Conversely, where under the pressure of the class adversary, as a result of the internal struggle or of a departure from the correct class line the leading role of the party is weakened and is reduced to nought, the revolutionary force may well be threatened with defeat.

* * *

Attacking the CPSU backfired badly for Gorbachev. He had made a dangerous assumption: that the liberals and nationalists he promoted would give him the political support denied him by the communists, thus allowing him to realize his dreams of a mixed economy with a welfare state and political pluralism. In fact, these elements wanted to go much further than Gorbachev. They did not want Nordic-style social democracy; they wanted full-scale neoliberal capitalism of the Milton Friedman variety. Soon enough they turned against Gorbachev and started looking for other means to promote their cause, stirring up nationalism and unrest, building openly pro-capitalist networks and attracting concrete support from the West.

To the extent that economic and political reform were necessary, they could only have been successfully carried out under the leadership of the CPSU, an organization which, for all its faults, counted among its number the most dedicated and capable people in Soviet society. Contrasting Gorbachev's approach with that of Deng Xiaoping, Allen Lynch writes,

> Where Deng defended the Chinese Communist Party, the only organization that integrated the country as a whole, Gorbachev undermined the Soviet Communist Party without having in place an alternative and legitimate system of authority. . . . Deng would not risk experiments with the political monopoly of the Chinese Communist Party, although he proved much defter in establishing his leadership over it than did Gorbachev over the Soviet counterpart. And when Deng saw that discussion of Western democracy implied a challenge to Communist Party rule, he drew a bright red line; again, this was very much unlike Gorbachev, who ended his tenure torn between a Soviet Communist Party that he could not abandon and democratic forces that he would not embrace.

Having debilitated and alienated the Communist Party and having failed to win enduring approval of the intelligentsia that he had courted so assiduously, Gorbachev found himself isolated and unpopular. 'Denied political recognition and support at home', Zubok wrote bitterly, Gorbachev 'increasingly looked for it abroad, from Western leaders.' In the United States, Britain and West Germany, Gorbachev was feted as a great hero, and his response was to start adopting the language and politics that went down best in these countries: the language and politics of imperialism. Class struggle increasingly gave way to 'universal values'. Defence of the socialist heartlands gave way to pacifism. The longstanding concept of nuclear parity was dropped. In the final insult to socialist morality and internationalism, Gorbachev responded to the US request that the Soviet Union participate in the 1991 Gulf War by saying, 'I want to emphasize that we would like to be by your side in any situation. We want decisions to be made that will strengthen, not undermine, the authority of the United States' (quoted in Chernyaev 2000).

CHAPTER 6

Things Fall Apart (1989–91)

Many of us aspire to change the world for the better: you are among the few who have successfully done so.

– British Conservative Prime Minister John Major
to Mikhail Gorbachev, December 1991

Many people had high hopes for Gorbachev. In the first year or two on the job, there was a sense that the new General Secretary had the energy, creativity and commitment to lead the USSR out of economic stagnation and political disillusionment. By 1987, this initial excitement had waned, replaced with apprehension and worry. Economic growth, which in 1985 had been relatively slow, was by now anaemic, and the Communist Party was being actively marginalized. Many Party members and leaders started to wonder – some openly – if perestroika and glasnost were really such great ideas.

Nonetheless, the years 1987 to 1989 were still approximately *business as usual* in the USSR. People went to work, received their salaries, and enjoyed an acceptable standard of living. Economist David Kotz (2017) notes, 'the increasingly radical economic reforms of the late 1980s were disruptive, but economic growth continued at 2.2% per year from 1985 to '89. The Soviet economy did not have a single year of economic contraction over the whole period from 1950 to 1989.' However, from 1989 the winds of change picked up pace and gathered into a hurricane, the destructive power of which caught the masses off-guard and ultimately turned Soviet socialism to rubble.

By 1989, Gorbachev and his allies had completed their quiet coup, consolidating their power, removing enemies and rivals from positions of influence, and paving an open road for their 'restructuring'. In the Congress of People's Deputies, they now had a legislative body that was more or less free from the reins of socialist sanity that might otherwise be applied by 'conservatives' and 'hardliners'. The media had succeeded in creating a political atmosphere in which any criticism of perestroika was simply 'Stalinism' – a word whose usage had come to imply acceptance of the most hyperbolic McCarthyite propaganda.

The leadership used its new-found freedom to start implementing much more radical reforms, closing down the central planning agencies altogether, liberalizing prices, establishing market-based trade between the republics, and forcing state enterprises to survive or die in the open market. Many large enterprises were sold off at bargain-basement prices to budding capitalist opportunists. These abrupt, hasty and sweeping reforms were meant to introduce 'dynamism' into the economy; to leverage the supposedly dormant creative spirit of the Soviet people; to incentivize innovation and quality. Judged against their purported intent, the reforms were spectacularly unsuccessful, leading to the first recession in Soviet history and to terrible shortages of low-margin and previously subsidized products. As Kotz and Weir (1997) put it, 'the Soviet economy moved from a condition of severe problems to one of crisis'.

At the turn of the decade, the economy was in free fall. With discontent rising and the CPSU in forced retreat, other political forces started to rise. Nationalist separatists in the non-Russian republics were able to prey on rising popular anxiety over the economy. Russian demagogues started denouncing the unequal relationship within the union whereby a wealthier Russia helped to sustain living conditions in central Asia. 'Radical reformers' like Boris Yeltsin, strongly backed by Western media and money, stirred up mass discontent. Strikes became a feature of everyday life. The threat of counter-revolution, previously unthinkable, became all too real.

* * *

By 1989–90, the economic and social situation was starting to deteriorate at a dangerous pace, and the effects became visible and impossible to ignore. With lots of cash chasing very few products, the lines outside the shops got longer and longer, and commodity rationing was stepped up. All this served to create a sense of crisis, and struck a mortal blow to the government's credibility.

The following year, per capita GDP fell by around 15 per cent; the reformers' blind faith in the inherent corrective power of the market turned out to be misplaced; investment collapsed. Net fixed investment *fell by 21 per cent* in 1990.

Price liberalization inevitably led to speculation and inflation, which in turn exacerbated the acute shortages of everyday consumer items, in particular food. This had its most visible manifestation in the notorious shopping queues that were much talked about in the West and which were, ironically, used as examples of the failure of socialism. Keeran and Kenny (2004) observe, 'Private hoarding by consumers and, more important, public hoarding by republics and cities, spread dramatically, first with respect to food, then other consumer goods. Empty food shelves, the most glaring and most resented shortage, drew sharp public anger and had widespread political, psychological, and economic results.'

In 1989 and 1990, socialist allies in Europe were transformed overnight into pro-Western capitalist regimes, leading to further imbalances in the Soviet economy – the USSR had long enjoyed a symbiotic trade relationship with the German Democratic Republic, Poland, Bulgaria, Hungary, Romania and Czechoslovakia – as well as to a growing popular perception that the writing was on the wall for European socialism. Much frustrated by the economic crisis and falling prey to the cynical demagoguery of Yeltsin and his coterie who blamed all problems on socialist planning and the 'privileged bureaucracy', coal miners carried out strikes on an unprecedented scale. Gorbachev had little choice but to go running to the Western banks, with which the Soviet Union quickly worked up a sizeable debt.

Yegor Ligachev, the most prominent 'hardliner' (i.e. socialist) on the scene at the time, describes the dangerously unstable situation of 1990–91,

> The consumer goods shortage hit hard, and people's dissatisfaction mounted. In the republics of the former Soviet Union, separatist tendencies gained strength. The Soviet Union's position in the international arena was weakened. There arose in the country political movements that aimed at eliminating the Soviet system and creating a society on the western model. Relying on active support from foreign powers, the shadow economy, the 'elite' of the creative intelligentsia, and a portion of the state apparatus, by means of deceit and demagoguery, especially regarding the non-existent privileges of the nomenklatura [high-level party appointees], these movements were able to enlist the support of a certain segment of society.

* * *

> Our people have never rejected socialism. They were simply deceived by demagoguery and false promises.
>
> – Gennady Zyuganov (1997)

As bad as things got, the Soviet working class was still not won over *en masse* to the putative delights of capitalism. Even with the level of ideological deterioration that had taken place, even with the pernicious influence of a hostile, anti-communist media, Soviet workers remained proud of the world-shaking achievements of their forebears and of the USSR's record of solidarity with the global anti-colonial and anti-imperialist struggle. These were for the most part educated people whose loyalty could not so easily be bought. Many understood that the luxurious and carefree lifestyle portrayed in Hollywood movies had its counterpart in the suffering and exploitation of the Western working classes and the oppressed masses of the developing world. Indeed, there were many in the grassroots of the CPSU that were highly critical of the retreat from Marxism-Leninism, but these were precisely the elements that were disenfranchised under Gorbachev's glasnost.

Facing a nationalist-separatist challenge throughout the federation, the Soviet government decided in late 1990 to hold a referendum on the preservation of the USSR – the only referendum in Soviet history. On March 17, 1991, Soviet people across the union went to the polls to give a yes-or-no answer to the question: 'Do you consider it necessary to preserve the Union of Soviet Socialist Republics as a renewed federation of equal sovereign republics, which will fully guarantee the rights and freedoms of all nationalities?' The vote was boycotted by the governing bodies in Lithuania, Latvia, Estonia, Armenia, Moldova and Georgia, but in the rest of the country turnout was 80 per cent, with 147 million total votes cast. The result was an overwhelming majority in favour of maintaining the USSR: 78 per cent voted in favour.

Interestingly, the proportion of 'yes' votes was slightly lower in Russia (73 per cent) and Ukraine (71 per cent) but extremely high in the Central Asian republics (over 94 per cent in Uzbekistan, Azerbaijan, Turkmenistan, Kazakhstan, Kyrgyzstan and Tajikistan) and Belarus. This reflects a growing eurocentrism and reactionary nationalism within Russia and Ukraine that resented sharing a state with 'backward' and 'burdensome' Asians – a prejudice that Yeltsin and others played to. Realizing that there was precious little support for dismantling socialism in the Central Asian and Caucasian republics, and reasoning that an independent Russia constituted a more promising environment for the type of free-market capitalism he had in mind, Yeltsin led the drive towards greater autonomy for Russia. He is on record as saying, in 1990, 'I soon understood that there would be no radical reforms at an all-Union level . . . and so I thought to myself: If the reforms cannot be carried out at that level, why not try in Russia?' (Quoted in Keeran and Kenny 2004)

Even the lead capitalist restorationists did not feel confident enough to talk about getting rid of socialism altogether, because they knew they would never get a popular mandate for their plans. Yeltsin did not talk openly about capitalism, only about accelerating the reforms, removing the privileges of the 'nomenklatura' and ending the CPSU's monopoly on power.

Soviet workers wanted to maintain and improve socialism and maintain the union. The USSR's dissolution at the end of 1991 was in that sense profoundly anti-democratic. However, crisis and confusion were so entrenched that, while people might *vote* for socialism, most were not mobilized to *fight* for it.

* * *

In spite of their catchphrases about 'democratization', the anti-communists had absolutely no interest in the will of the Soviet people. Instead, they were intent on pushing through their programme of capitalist restoration by any means necessary. Thanks to perestroika and glasnost, they had both the economic incentive and political leverage to dismantle socialism, break up the USSR and send its people hurtling into an economic and social crisis of untold proportions.

The major constituency pushing for capitalism was, to use Kotz and Weir's terminology, *the party-state elite* – mid-level officials and enterprise managers who had taken advantage of their extensive connections and new-found economic freedoms to win control of assets and engage in trade and finance. Dissolution of the USSR offered such people (together with the bigger players in the underground economy) the promise of a completely deregulated trade environment in which they would be able to get unimaginably rich, albeit at the expense of the remaining 99 per cent of the population. Kotz and Weir discuss the mechanics of how these people came into money, and why the destruction of socialism was so close to their hearts,

> The decree on foreign trade of 1988 opened an important means to get rich. The Soviet Union's low controlled prices made many Soviet goods, particularly oil and metals, potentially lucrative export items for anyone who could get hold of them. After this decree opened up foreign trade to private firms, import-export companies were formed, in the legal form of cooperatives, which soon began to conduct a partly legal, partly illegal, and very profitable export trade. Over three thousand such firms were formed. . . . By 1990–91 a new group of private capitalists had developed and was getting rich mainly through connections with the outside world. . . . Any turn away from the emerging pro-capitalist direction of change, toward either a return to the building of a reformed socialism, or an effort to bring back the pre-perestroika system, would threaten the basis of their lucrative economic endeavours. Proceeding to capitalism was essential to the survival of their new businesses.

This pro-capitalist constituency had money. And money, for the first time, had become a significant factor in the Soviet political scene. 'Free elections' turned out not to be so free in the case of the Congress of People's Deputies, where money bought high-profile campaigns and extensive media coverage. This was an unfamiliar environment for the silent majority in the Communist Party that had been brought up to believe that political leadership was a responsibility and honour earned through service to the people, not paid for with ill-gotten gains. This change, together with Gorbachev's insistence on dropping quotas for working-class representation, meant – as Sam Marcy wrote – that 'a striking change occurred in the percentage of deputies who were workers, collective farmers and office employees: this dropped from 45.9% of the 1984 Supreme Soviet to only 23.1% in 1989'. The counterpart to this was the monumental increase in the representation of management and intelligentsia.

With the formation of the overtly anti-communist 'Democratic Russia' movement in January 1990, the pro-capitalist elements joined forces and consolidated around a political vehicle that offered the quickest possible route to their chosen destination. Democratic Russia candidates managed to win a plurality of seats in the Russian parliamentary elections of March 1990, including several key Soviets (Moscow and Leningrad among them). Democratic Russia also played the major role in electing Boris Yeltsin as Chair of the Russian Parliament in May 1990. By this time, Yeltsin had become recognized as the undisputed leader of the anti-communist opposition. He resigned from the Communist Party in June 1990, realizing that his differences with Gorbachev were insurmountable. Gorbachev, for all his ineptitude and liberalism, still hoped to keep the USSR together and maintain some elements of socialism – for example, the welfare state. As Gorbachev put it on June 22, 1987,

> We are well aware of our weaknesses and unresolved problems, but neither can we forget the fact that socialism has given every one of us the right to work and to an education, free medical service, and accessible housing. These are genuine values in our society which provide social protection for the individual today and for the future. (Interview cited in Marcy 1990)

Yeltsin and his cohort wanted to press ahead with 'shock therapy' neoliberalism and had lost patience with Gorbachev. Yeltsin's bold statements against the communist 'conservatives', his nationalist demagoguery, and his carefully nurtured (and entirely inaccurate) image of incorruptibility won him phenomenally high approval ratings from 1989 onwards. The reactionaries placed their hopes in his shaking hands.

The imperialist countries made it perfectly clear which side they were on, openly stating that any support for the Russian economy via the international banks would be predicated on an economic programme of large-scale privatization and deregulation. Within this framework, 'saving Russia' meant embracing the most brutal neoliberalism.

* * *

Reagan's vocal support to 'pro-democracy' movements in Europe, along with Gorbachev's clear indications that the Soviet Union would not intervene militarily to protect its allies, gave a tremendous impetus to the project of capitalist restoration across the region. With communists almost entirely sidelined in Moscow, pro-capitalist and pro-perestroika elements in the rest of the Warsaw Treaty zone were emboldened. Well-funded Western-backed organizations were able to use sophisticated marketing and radical posturing in order to leverage popular dissatisfaction into powerful movements for counter-revolutionary change. In the words of Margot Honecker, people came to believe they could 'join together the glittering world of commodities under capitalism and the social security of socialism' ('Interview with Margot Honecker', 2015).

In August 1989, following extended negotiations between the Polish government and the 'Solidarity' union movement (a grateful recipient of bountiful CIA funds and papal support), leading anti-communist Tadeusz Mazowiecki became prime minister and Poland became the first of the European socialist states to fall.

The most dramatic and symbolic events in Europe were in the German Democratic Republic, where large demonstrations were held, initially calling for greater democracy and bemoaning a stagnant economy. Anti-communist elements saw their opportunity and started steering the demonstrations towards a demand for German reunification – thereby implying that the GDR authorities were responsible for the ongoing division of the country. As an aside, it is worth noting that the basic history of German partition and the Berlin Wall continues to be wilfully misrepresented. In the negotiations over the status of post-war Europe at Yalta and Potsdam, the Soviet Union and its allies in the German Communist Party (KPD) had pushed strongly for a unified German state that would have multi-party elections, that would be prevented from rearmament and that would be committed to neutrality. This approach considered both the wishes of the German people and the Soviet Union's need to avoid another major war. Anxious to maintain a military foothold in Germany, the United States and Britain worked with right-wing forces in the western zone (including many former Nazis) to set up a separate state in western Germany: the Federal German Republic (FRG), established in May 1949. It was only then that the GDR was set up as a separate, socialist state. The border in Berlin then became the nexus for covert actions by Western imperialism against the socialist bloc (it should be recalled that, throughout this era, US-led capitalism was waging a horrifically violent global crusade against progressive forces, from Cuba to Korea, from Vietnam to Indonesia, from Guatemala to Congo). The constant threat of war was the major reason for the construction of the Berlin Wall. Margot Honecker notes:

> The Political Advisory Committee, which was the governing body of the Warsaw Treaty states, decided in the summer of 1961 to close the border in Berlin and the western state border after they decided a military confrontation could no longer be ruled out. I do not think that one can call the prevention of a possible third world war a mistake.

The counter-revolution in the GDR picked up pace rapidly after the Hungarian state – by now well advanced along the road of its own version of perestroika – tore down its border with Austria. Much encouraged by the Western authorities, several hundred East Germans took the opportunity to cross the Austria-Hungary border and make their way to the FRG. This created a panic situation in East Berlin. In November 1989, crowds of Germans on both sides started dismantling the wall. Given the 'facts on the ground' created by the Hungarian border opening and the Soviet refusal to intervene, the authorities in the GDR – by now vulnerable and indecisive, with the Erich Honecker leadership sidelined – chose not to prevent the fall of the wall. Within a year, the GDR ceased to exist.

By 1990, Communist parties had been removed from power in Poland, Germany, Hungary, Czechoslovakia, Bulgaria and Romania. Albania would soon follow suit, and Yugoslavia was descending into a series of nationalist secessions and terrible wars. The Warsaw Treaty of collective security was disbanded in February 1991. A few months later the Council for Mutual Economic Assistance (popularly known as *Comecon*) was dissolved.

The collapse of the socialist states in Central and Eastern Europe served to significantly increase the pressure on Soviet socialism. At the most practical level, there had been a tight economic integration between the CMEA countries: a similar economic model meant that economic planning could be partly internationalized. The sudden disappearance of the USSR's key trading partners meant a vertiginous decline in imports and exports, leading to sudden shortages of various essential goods.

* * *

National tensions started to escalate in the Gorbachev period, fuelled to a significant degree by Gorbachev's insensitivity to the national question and his purge against those not toeing the perestroika line. Breaking with the tradition that the Politburo and

Central Committee should have representation from all the republics, Gorbachev oversaw a 'russification' of the central bodies, feeding into resentment and rising complaints about Russian chauvinism. For example, the highly capable Azeri leader Heydar Aliyev, promoted by Andropov to the position of First Deputy Premier of the Soviet Union, was unceremoniously kicked out of the Politburo in 1987. Nikolai Baibakov, another senior Party leader from Azerbaijan, was fired in 1985. Dinmukhamed Kunayev, longstanding Party head in Kazakhstan and a full Politburo member for 16 years, was also dismissed as a result of his ambivalence regarding perestroika. He was replaced as Kazakh Party chairman by Gennady Kolbin – a Russian who had never lived in Kazakhstan. Kolbin's rise prompted rioting on the streets of the capital, Almaty (then known as Alma-Ata).

The sorry state of affairs in the Soviet economy gave a further stimulus to nationalist separatist movements, particularly in the western republics. Between March and May 1990, national separatists dominated the elections to the Supreme Soviet in Lithuania, Estonia and Latvia; all three republics promptly declared independence. Although Gorbachev opposed the independence of the Baltic states, he chose to accept it rather than enforce the union and thereby invoke the ire of his new-found friends on the international scene: US president George H.W. Bush and German chancellor Helmut Kohl.

By late 1990, with the writing on the wall for the union, the remaining republics had declared 'sovereignty' (not independence), asserting control over their own territory and the economic resources within it. The first republic to quit the USSR was Russia in June 1990. This was an unconstitutional move made by Yeltsin. It was motivated primarily by the impatience of the neoliberal hawks, who wanted to go faster than Gorbachev down the capitalist road. The other republics responded in kind. Kotz and Weir write that the passage of the sovereignty law in Russia had an immediate and profound effect on the other republics, transforming the nature of the nationalist impulses coursing through the republics. However much ethnic Russians might have dominated the Soviet system, the structure of the Union at least provided some safeguards and powers, as well as significant economic benefits, to the non-Russian republics. For example, Russia's plentiful raw materials had been provided cheaply throughout the Soviet Union. Now the Russian Republic was asserting its right to control its own natural resources and their disposition. The leaderships of the republics which had previously been relatively quiet now immediately passed sovereignty resolutions. By August 1990 sovereignty resolutions had been passed by Uzbekistan, Moldavia, Ukraine, Turkmenistan, and Tajikistan. By October even loyal Kazakhstan followed suit as well.

The breakup of the integrated economic system had an acute economic impact. The entire Soviet economy was based on Union-wide integration and division of labour, with the supply chain managed through central planning. Textbooks might be manufactured in one state, dairy products in another, steel rods and industrial plastics in another. It's not difficult to understand how the sudden disintegration of this system would have contributed to economic disaster.

* * *

By mid-1991, the confidence of the anti-socialist opposition was growing by the day. On July 20, Yeltsin issued a decree banning the Russian branch of the Communist Party from operating in government offices and workplaces within the Russian Republic (Fein 1991). It was perfectly obvious to all concerned that this was a power grab aimed at finishing off the CPSU and establishing Russia as an independent (capitalist) country.

Seeing their country hurtling towards oblivion – and recognizing that Gorbachev lacked either the will or the ability to save it – a group of high-level Soviet officials organized themselves to take control of the country and establish a state of emergency, with a view to pausing the reforms and pursuing all measures to prevent the dissolution of the USSR. These officials organized themselves under the name *State Committee on the State of Emergency* (SCSE). Among them were some of the government's top leaders, including Gennady Yanayev (Vice President), Valentin Pavlov (Premier), Boris Pugo (Interior Minister) and Dmitry Yazov (Defence Minister). They were joined by army commander-in-chief Valentin Varennikov and KGB head Vladimir Kryuchkov.

On August 18, with Gorbachev on holiday in the Crimea, tanks moved into Moscow and a state of emergency was declared. The SCSE issued its *Appeal to the Soviet People* on August 19. Their appeal stated, 'There have emerged extremist forces which have adopted a course toward liquidation of the Soviet Union, the collapse of the state and the seizure of power at any price' and denounced the economic reforms which had caused 'a sharp drop in the living standards of the overwhelming majority of the population and the flowering of speculation and the shadow economy' (cited in Keeran and Kenny 2004). The statement promised to clamp down on the emerging capitalist class and to initiate a country-wide discussion on the future of the federation.

However, the SCSE leadership quickly developed an acute case of cold feet, dropping its plan to storm the Russian parliament and showing no willingness to use force in support of its aims. They did not even perform the most basic preparatory task of cutting off Yeltsin's telephone. Gao Di, chief editor of *People's Daily* and high-ranking member of the Chinese Communist Party, wrote at the time that the SCSE 'should simply have arrested Yeltsin and Gorbachev before they did anything else, just as we did the Gang of Four. . . . You do not ask a tiger politely for his skin – either you kill him, or he will kill you!' (Quoted in Shambaugh 2008)

On August 21, KGB head Vladimir Kryuchkov flew to Crimea in an attempt to persuade Gorbachev to give his stamp of approval to the SCSE and to join them in forestalling Yeltsin's plans. Here is Keeran and Kenny's summary of what happened:

> Gorbachev would not meet them. At 2:30 am on August 22nd Gorbachev returned to Moscow on the presidential plane along with the Russian Republic's Vice President Rutskoi (Yeltsin's ally, who had arrived in Foros on another plane), and Kryuchkov. Kryuchkov had agreed to join Gorbachev on the presidential plane, on the basis of a promise he would speak as an equal with Gorbachev. On landing, however, Kryuchkov was arrested by Soviet authorities. Back in Moscow, Gorbachev resumed formal power, though his real power was fast slipping into the hands of Yeltsin. At 9 am on August 22 the Soviet Ministry of Defence decided to withdraw its troops from Moscow, and the bizarre drama came to an end.

All in all, it was a thoroughly inept and half-hearted operation. As Gennady Zyuganov, leader of the Communist Party of the Russian Federation, remarked many years later in a statement on the death of Gennady Yanayev, 'If they had acted much more decisively, our unified country would have been preserved' ('Leader of failed coup dies', 2010). Ligachev (1996) recalled, 'They courageously attempted to preserve the Soviet Union. If they are to be criticized, it is for their inconsistency and indecision.'

Yeltsin was quick to exploit the events to further his own position and accelerate the overthrow of socialism. The pro-capitalist leadership within the Russian parliament immediately denounced the coup attempt and called their supporters to defend Moscow's White House (the base of the parliament), where the speakers called openly and defiantly for ending socialism without further delay. Aleksandr Rutskoi, Russian vice president, shouted to the crowd: 'Either we shall live like the rest of the world, or we shall continue to call ourselves the socialist choice and the Communist prospect, and live like pigs' (Kotz and Weir 1997). Yakovlev joined the protests, along with Eduard Shevardnadze, who would later become the (thoroughly reactionary) Georgian head of state.

The image of Yeltsin sitting atop a tank outside the Russian parliament served as powerful fuel for his self-promotion engine, appearing on TV screens and front pages across the country and around the world. In the mainstream narrative, he was a courageous democrat, a hero of all that is good and pure. All this set Yeltsin on an accelerated track to seize full power in Russia and pull the plug on the Soviet Union.

* * *

With the SCSE defeated and its members imprisoned, events moved at lightning pace. On August 23, Yeltsin pushed through the suspension of the Russian branch of the Communist Party. On August 24, Gorbachev dissolved the CPSU Central Committee and resigned from his role as General Secretary (maintaining his position as President of the country). A day later, Yeltsin ordered the transfer of the Russian Communist Party's property to the Russian Parliament. The Soviet flag outside the Kremlin was replaced with the Russian flag. Nothing meaningful remained of the Soviet state.

In early November, Yeltsin issued Decree No. 169, banning the CPSU altogether. He sought to justify this move on the basis that 'it has become evident that as long as the CPSU structures exist, there can be no guarantee against one more putsch or a coup' (quoted in Berliner 1991). This was thoroughly disingenuous, given that his executive order restricting the Party's activities in Russia was one of the key factors precipitating the SCSE's attempt to restore socialist governance. However, there was by now nobody left in the leadership with the courage or strength to sabotage Yeltsin's bourgeois bulldozer.

Yeltsin ignored the negotiations for a new union agreement and moved purposefully towards declaring Russian independence. On December 8, he met with the Ukrainian and Belorussian presidents, Leonid Kravchuk and Stanislav Shushkevich, ostensibly for informal discussions. At this meeting, the presidents and their advisers drafted a document (known as the Belavezha Accords) announcing – with absolutely no legal authority – the dissolution of the Soviet Union: 'The USSR, as a subject of international law and a geopolitical reality, is ceasing its existence' ('Declarations by 3 Republic Leaders', 1991). Shushkevich's memory of the discussion gives some idea as to how much attention was paid to the nuances of constitutional law: 'Yeltsin said, "Would you agree for the Soviet Union to end its existence?" I said OK and Kravchuk said OK too' (Kendall 2011).

Even Gorbachev was shocked at the arbitrary and sudden nature of this declaration. On December 9, 1991, he stated,

> The fate of the multinational state cannot be determined by the will of the leaders of three republics. The question should be decided only by constitutional means with the participation of all sovereign states and taking into account the will of all their citizens. . . . The hastiness with which the document appeared is also of serious concern. It was not discussed by the populations nor by the Supreme Soviets of the republics in whose name it was signed. Even worse, it appeared at the moment when the draft treaty for a Union of Sovereign States, drafted by the USSR State Council, was being discussed by the parliaments of the republics. (Quoted in Gorbachev 2000)

There was little support for Soviet dissolution in the Central Asian and Caucasian republics, but it was not conceivable to carry the Soviet

Union on without its most populous and prominent component, namely Russia. The Belavezha Accords were ratified a week later by the leaders of the remaining republics. Gorbachev's resignation finally came on December 25, 1991. With no legal precedent or constitutional framework, Yeltsin simply transferred the Soviet state bodies and property to Russia, and on December 31, the Soviet Union formally ceased to exist. It was not a revolution; it was a coup. A great country was removed from the map, against the wishes of the majority of its people, by opportunist and conniving leaders. It was nothing short of a tragedy.

CHAPTER 7

Restoration of Capitalism

> There can be no more tragic spectacle in the history of humanity than that of a defeated revolution. When the revolt of the slaves in Rome was defeated, thousands were nailed to crosses on the roadside. This should give us an idea of what a defeated revolution is. . . . There was also the dreadful slaughter of workers after the defeat of the Paris Commune [in 1871]. This, too, should give us an idea of what a defeated revolution is. History teaches us that a defeated revolution has to pay an extraordinary toll in blood. The victorious ruling class demands payment for the anxiety it experienced, for all the interests that were affected, or that were threatened. But it not only demands payment for present debts; it also seeks to collect, in blood, payment for future debts. It tries to annihilate the revolution down to its very roots.
>
> – Fidel Castro, 1961

> Question: What did capitalism accomplish in one year that communism could not do in seventy years?
> Answer: Make communism look good.
>
> – A joke circulating in Russia in 1992

With the burden of Gorbachev's social democratic fantasies lifted from his shoulders, Yeltsin went to work on behalf of his major constituency: the most corrupt and unscrupulous sections of the Russian nouveau riche, along with US finance capital. The goal was to totally wipe out the economic foundations of socialism and create a fully liberalized economy where capital would be free to reproduce without fear of restriction or regulation; an economic environment purpose-built for foreign investors, speculators, bankers and gangsters.

But, as Gregory Isaacs put it, 'a rich man's heaven is a poor man's hell'. The welfare state was all but wiped out. The neoliberal economic advisers hired by Yeltsin – led by Jeffrey Sachs – mandated an end to price controls, meaning that the prices of even the most essential commodities skyrocketed overnight. Unemployment went from practically zero to over 12 per cent within a few months. Asset-stripping reached dizzy new heights. Privatization, deregulation and corruption were the order of the day, as production, government spending, earnings and even life expectancy plummeted. In the first half of the 1990s, male life expectancy dropped from 65 to 57 – an unprecedented fall in any context other than full-scale war.

As funding dried up, the healthcare infrastructure collapsed, and the peoples of the former Soviet Union were subjected to epidemics of poverty-fuelled diseases not seen for many decades. The *Los Angeles Times* reported in 1994, 'Azerbaijan has had a tenfold increase in measles, Uzbekistan suffered an outbreak of polio and typhoid fever has reappeared in Russia. Tuberculosis and syphilis are widespread, and the incidence of such children's diseases as whooping cough and German measles has increased sharply' (Efron 1994). Russia witnessed its first cholera epidemic since the 19th century.

In the first few years following the collapse of the Soviet Union, Russian GDP and industrial production both contracted by more than 40 per cent. As Kotz and Weir (1997) note, 'By comparison, in the United States the four-year economic contraction in 1929–33, which brought the American economy to the low point of the Great Depression, entailed a decline in gross national product of 30 per cent.' Needless to say, wages followed suit, and the Soviet people started to suffer serious poverty for the first time in many decades. According to a World Bank report on the 'transition economies' (all the former socialist countries of Central Europe, Eastern Europe and Central Asia), the number of people living on less than four dollars per day increased from 14 million in 1989 to 147 million in the mid-1990s. In Russia this corresponded to an increase from two per cent to 44 per cent; in Ukraine from one per cent to 63 per cent; in Central Asia from 6.5 per cent to 53 per cent.

It took around 15 years for Russian GDP to recover to 1990 levels – during which period China's GDP increased by around 300 per cent. Even after GDP had returned to 1990 levels, the obscene levels of inequality meant that millions of Russians still lived with a level of poverty that had not been seen in the Soviet Union since the Second World War. New problems emerged, most noticeably homelessness (including youth homelessness), drug addiction, social alienation and prostitution, all of which remain endemic in Russia today. Yegor Ligachev (1996) lamented the tragedy of post-Soviet Russia:

> During the years of Soviet power, a person was judged, not by his bag of loot, but by his labour, and lofty moral principles were reinforced: patriotism, internationalism, collectivism, industry, honour, justice. Now, all that is being stamped out of people's consciousness and the historical connection is being broken. The current authorities and the mass media are encouraging the cult of gain, grovelling to the rich, contempt for the poor, speculation, hard drinking, prostitution and savage individualism. . . .
>
> All measures of development have taken a sharp downturn except mortality and crime – which are rising steeply. This is understandable. The property created by and belonging to the workers is being stolen, society is rife with alcoholism, and the number of unemployed and homeless is growing. The authorities cannot fight the very people they depend upon, that is, the speculators and the corrupt apparatus. . . .
>
> In the Soviet era . . . you could walk through any town at night

> without concern for your life; now murders and robberies are committed in broad daylight.

The Soviet collapse also had a disastrous effect on cultural and social life. Michael Parenti (2001) points out that

> Subsidies for the arts and literature have been severely cut. Symphony orchestras have disbanded or taken to playing at block parties and other minor occasions. The communist countries used to produce inexpensive but quality editions of classical and contemporary authors and poets, including ones from Latin America, Asia and Africa. These have been replaced by second-rate, mass-market publications from the West.

With widespread poverty and yawning inequality came xenophobic scapegoating, violent crime and domestic abuse. No wonder a majority of Russians regret the collapse.

Ironically, even some leading Western journalists now recognize that socialism offered a far better deal for ordinary people than neoliberal capitalism. Adam Taylor, writing in *The Washington Post* in 2016, admitted,

> The planned economy of the vast Soviet Union offered financial stability. In the immediate aftermath of its 1991 crash, it quickly became apparent that Russia's new market economy would offer a rocky ride. Economic reforms quickly had a harsh effect on general living standards. The rouble became almost worthless. Corruption was rampant. A deeply flawed privatization programme helped put much of the country's economy in the hands of an entrenched and often shady oligarchy.

It is now widely believed that US-led finance capital knowingly directed the post-Soviet Russian economy into disaster so as to: 1) thoroughly wipe out the economic roots of socialism by replacing it with gangster anarcho-capitalism; and 2) to prevent the Russian Federation from becoming a serious competitor to US post-Cold War hegemony.

* * *

Yeltsin in power confirmed what every thinking person suspected: he had not the slightest interest in democracy. The brutal neoliberalism imposed on the Russian people could never have enjoyed popular legitimacy – how then to win widespread support for the dismantling of social welfare and the transfer of the state's assets to a bunch of bureaucrats and crooks? Therefore, a corrupt, plutocratic political system was installed that openly favoured the enormously wealthy and that actively excluded the poor. In stark contrast to their role during Soviet times, trade unions were barred from political activity. Pro-communist and anti-Yeltsin media were routinely banned.

By autumn 1993, Yeltsin was facing serious opposition even within the Russian parliament, a majority of whose members were appalled by the results of the neoliberal 'reform' and Yeltsin's use of extraordinary executive powers to push his programme through. A constitutional crisis arose when Yeltsin decided to put an end to the pesky parliamentary opposition by dissolving the legislature (unconstitutional dissolution seems by this point to have become something of a habit). The parliament responded by denouncing Yeltsin's actions, impeaching him and declaring Vice President Aleksandr Rutskoi acting president. The crisis was only 'resolved' when Yeltsin ordered the army to storm the Supreme Soviet and arrest the parliamentary leaders that opposed him. Quite the democratic transformation. Stephen Cohen, who has studied Russia for the better part of a half century, writes,

> The most influential pro-Yeltsin intellectuals were neither coincidental

> fellow travellers nor real democrats. Since the late 1980s they had insisted that free-market economics and large-scale private property would have to be imposed on Russian society by an 'iron hand' regime using 'anti-democratic measures'. Like the property-seeking elites, they saw Russia's newly elected legislatures as an obstacle. Admirers of Chile's Augusto Pinochet, they said of Yeltsin: 'Let him be a dictator!' Not surprisingly, they cheered (along with the US government and mainstream media) when he used tanks to destroy Russia's popularly elected parliament in 1993.

Three years later, in 1996, the Russian presidential elections were almost certainly fixed – with backing from the United States – so as to maintain Yeltsin in power at the expense of the Communist Party candidate, Gennady Zyuganov.

Yeltsin had portrayed himself as the 'father of Russian democracy'; he turned out to be its leading assassin.

* * *

> The destruction of socialism in the USSR . . . inflicted terrible damage on all peoples of the world and created a bad situation for the Third World in particular.
>
> – Fidel Castro

The importance of the USSR's role as a counterweight to US/NATO imperialism was made achingly clear by the series of imperialist wars that took place during and after the Soviet demise. Symbolic of this shifting power balance is Saddam Hussein's misplaced hope in early 1991 that Gorbachev would act to restrain US warmongering against Iraq. The Soviet Union was supposed to be a great power, a longstanding ally of Iraq, with its Armenian borders extending to within a couple of hundred kilometres of Iraqi Kurdistan. Gorbachev's government did nothing to protect Iraq from invasion by a predatory imperialist power on the other side of the world. It is rather difficult to imagine Stalin or Brezhnev presiding over such a mockery.

Horrifically destructive US-led wars soon followed in Yugoslavia, Afghanistan, Iraq (again), Libya and elsewhere. The campaign to destroy Syria's independence continues to this day. Without the existence of a socialist bloc in Europe, many states were left with no option but to swallow the brutal logic of neoliberalism, or what Samir Amin called 'the system of generalized monopolies'. Countries unwilling to play ball were subjected to the threat of violence. In the case of Yugoslavia, Afghanistan and Iraq, threat was converted into genocidal reality.

The balance of power in the world changed sharply, with the overwhelming majority of European socialist states being replaced by right-wing governments and incorporated into NATO (despite the promises made by the US and West Germany that there would be no eastward expansion of NATO). The economic crisis occasioned by the Soviet collapse also led to the demise of socialism in Mongolia.

With China yet to become the economic powerhouse it now is, underdeveloped countries in need of investment were left with no choice but to look to the United States, the Bretton Woods institutions and to commercial lenders. As a result, 'structural adjustment' became the order of the day, and many poorer countries were forced to accept the full neoliberal package of privatization, liberalization and austerity on a grand scale in exchange for loans that were needed to avert acute crises. Of the remaining socialist countries, Cuba, Vietnam and DPR Korea suffered particularly badly as a result of the sudden disappearance of the Soviet Union (and its friendly trade terms). It is a testament to the remarkable courage, creativity and vision of the Cuban, Vietnamese and Korean people that those countries have recovered from the shock of the early 1990s.

The collapse of the Soviet Union and European socialism could reasonably be described as the worst defeat suffered by the global working class in its history. It gave a lifeline to imperialism and set back the cause of human liberation by several decades.

CHAPTER 8

Looking Back and Moving Forward

> History does not progress in a straight line. It zigzags, steps back, and turns. The socialist phase of civilization has not managed to avoid those turns. Despite the temporary defeat of socialism in the Soviet Union, the twentieth century will go down in history for the destruction of the colonial system, the defeat of fascist tyranny, and the experiment in construction of a socialist society. On the basis of that history, humanity will eventually realize a breakthrough to a socially just society, one in which the individual will come to full fruition.
>
> – Yegor Ligachev (1996)

This book has explored in some detail the various factors – economic, political, ideological, military and cultural – that contributed to the collapse of the USSR and the dismantling of socialism in Europe. Although we are removed from the events discussed herewith by several decades, these questions are of no idle academic interest; they are essential components of the biggest political questions of our era: Has capitalism won? Is there any escape for humanity from brutal exploitation, inequality and underdevelopment? Is there a future in which the world's billions can truly exercise their free will, their humanity, liberated from both hunger and wage slavery?

For socialists, the major objective of studying the Soviet collapse is to improve our collective understanding of how to build, protect and develop socialism. This means, first of all, identifying the mistakes made by the Soviet leadership – this is the subjective factor. But the objective factor is also important: with the benefit of hindsight and the ever-increasing availability of historical data, we can piece together the complex geostrategic jigsaw that the USSR existed within. As such, we can more effectively identify similar patterns that confront socialist states now and in the future.

If the USSR had been able to overcome its economic stagnation from the 1970s onwards, there's every reason to believe it would still exist today. The manifold political and social problems that sprang up in the 1980s were fertilized by a latent dissatisfaction with regard to living standards. The USSR never caught up with the major imperialist powers in terms of technology and productivity, and from the late 1970s onwards the technology gap between the Soviet Union and the US grew sharply. All this conspired with an expanding military expenditure to ensure that many Soviet people didn't achieve material living standards matching those of their counterparts in North America and Western Europe. This situation was exacerbated by an increasing sense of alienation and the failure of the Communist Party to update its understanding and to keep the masses energized and engaged.

The Italian Marxist philosopher and historian Domenico Losurdo notes that, in the 1930s and '40s, the heavily centralized Soviet economy was working very well: 'The rapid development of modern industry was interwoven with the construction of a welfare state that guaranteed the economic and social rights of citizens in a way that was unprecedented.' However, after the period of frenetic building of socialism, followed by the war, followed by the reconstruction, came 'the transition from great historical crisis to a more normal period' in which 'the masses' enthusiasm and commitment to production and work weakened and then disappeared'. In its final few years, 'the Soviet Union was characterized by massive absenteeism and disengagement in the workplace: not only did production development stagnate, but there was no longer any application of the principle that Marx said drove socialism – remuneration according to the quantity and quality of work delivered.' At several points in the post-war period, Soviet leaders analysed these problems and proposed changes; various reforms were attempted, but none of them succeeded in breaking the trend towards stagnation.

What the Soviet leadership could have done better in terms of economics is a very difficult question to answer, and any hypotheses are entirely untestable. What we can usefully do is compare the Soviet approach with that taken by China and Vietnam, both of which took the road of economic reform in the same era as the USSR (China from 1978, Vietnam from 1986). In both cases, these reforms have had profoundly different results to those of Gorbachev's perestroika. For example, in the 40 years from 1978, China's economy expanded at an average of 9.5 per cent per year, resulting in a 35-fold increase. And, not coincidentally, the Communist parties of China and Vietnam still hold power. If 'the proof of the pudding is in the eating', then it must be concluded that these Asian socialist states made much better pudding, since the trajectory of their economies has been one of rapid growth, ever-improving living standards, and a narrowing of the gap with the advanced capitalist countries.

Martin Jacques (2012) states the case succinctly: 'We should think of China's communist regime quite differently from that of the USSR: it has, after all, succeeded where the Soviet Union failed.'

Gorbachev's reforms were implemented in an impatient, heavy-handed, top-down way, without consulting the people or attempting to collate feedback. His methodology was profoundly flawed. Soviet economists transitioned from central-planning dogma to neoliberal dogma, failing to come up with creative approaches that accurately took account of existing strengths and weaknesses.

Veteran Russian communist Gennady Zyuganov (1997) describes what Soviet economic reform *should* have looked like:

> A well-developed programme and precisely defined goals; a team of vigorous and highly intellectual reformers; a strong and effective system for controlling political phenomena; thoroughly developed and carefully considered methods of instituting the reforms; the mobilization of the mass media to explain the meaning, goals, and consequences of the reforms for the state as a whole and for the individual person in particular for the purpose of involving as much of the population as possible in the reform process; and the preservation and development of the structures, relations, functions, methods, and lifestyles that have earned the approval of the people.

Gorbachev didn't select people on the basis of competence or experience but on the basis of their uncritical support for his agenda. He didn't mobilize the existing, proven state structures, but sought to weaken them. The media wasn't used to unite the people behind a programme of development but to denigrate the Communist Party. The economic programme was incoherent and subject to sudden changes in direction. The masses were not invited to participate in any other way than doing what they were told. What followed was 'a parade of political arrogance, demagoguery, and dilettantism, which gradually overwhelmed and paralysed the country'.

Facing opposition to their economic programme, the Soviet top leadership in the Gorbachev era attacked the Communist Party, questioned its legitimacy, rewrote its history and sowed disillusion among the Soviet people. The attack on the Party was putatively carried out in the name of enhancing democracy, yet the results turned out to be profoundly anti-democratic. The Communist Party had been the major vehicle for promoting the needs and ideas of the working class; once it was sidelined, the workers had no obvious means of organizing in defence of their interests. This opened up a space for a pro-capitalist minority to dominate political power and, ultimately, break up the country and dismantle socialism. This result is of profound importance for shaping our understanding of socialist democracy, particularly in a global context of highly militarized imperialist hegemony.

Khrushchev and Gorbachev both thought that tarnishing the Soviet Communist Party's historical record would somehow help to rally forces for constructing a renewed socialism; they were wrong.

* * *

> One important reason for the disintegration of the Soviet Union and the collapse of the CPSU is the complete denial of the history of the Soviet Union, and the history of the CPSU, the denial of Lenin and other leading personalities, and historical nihilism confused the people's thoughts.
>
> – Xi Jinping

The issue of maintaining a workers' state and preventing the political domination of pro-capitalist 'liberals' is arguably the most important lesson to be learned from the collapse of the USSR. Even with ongoing economic difficulties and popular dissatisfaction, it's perfectly conceivable that Soviet socialism could have survived if the top leadership hadn't decided to abandon the project. Allen Lynch, a prominent researcher of Russian politics at the University of Virginia, speculates that, if Gorbachev's predecessor Yuri Andropov had lived another couple of decades (he died at the age of 69 after just one year as General Secretary of the CPSU), things might have been very different:

> Judging from Andropov's programmatic statements in 1982–83, as well as his long record at the summit of Soviet politics, there can be little doubt that he would not have countenanced anything remotely resembling Gorbachev's political reforms or that he would have hesitated to use force to stop public challenges to communist rule. Moreover, Andropov's networks in the Party, KGB, government and military were incomparably

> stronger than Gorbachev's and he might well have leveraged a viable coalition for piecemeal reform of the Soviet economy. While the long-term success of Andropov's economic vision may be questioned, it is entirely plausible that the Soviet Union – like Communist China – might still be with us. (Lynch 2012)

* * *

> Socialism will definitively remain the only real hope of peace and survival of our species. . . . Each people must adapt their strategy and revolutionary objectives to the concrete conditions of their own country; there are not two absolutely equal socialist revolutionary processes. From each of them, you can take the best experiences and learn from each of their most serious mistakes.
>
> – Fidel Castro

The lessons from the collapse of the Soviet Union must be thoroughly learned by the remaining (and future) socialist states as well as the global working class as a whole. In the current stage of history, where these states constitute a global minority and where they face a powerful ideological enemy that is determined to destabilize (and ultimately destroy) them, these lessons are broadly applicable. They form a key part of the great legacy that the Soviet experience leaves to the global progressive movement of humanity.

The Soviet project is by no means a historical relic; its experience is relevant and even crucial to contemporary politics. The heroic feats of the Soviet people live on in Cuba, China, Vietnam, Laos and Korea; in Venezuela, Bolivia and Kerala; in socialist-oriented and progressive states and movements around the world. Even in the territories of the former Soviet Union and the former socialist states in Europe, the memory of better times lives on – not least in the considerable defence and retention of Soviet achievements, traditions and forms in Belarus.

Their populations are starting, as Fidel Castro predicted they would, to regret the counter-revolution, to miss 'those orderly countries, where everyone had clothes, food, medicine, education, and there was no crime, no mafia'; they are beginning to 'realize the great historic mistake they made when they destroyed socialism' ('Fidel Castro In Vietnam', 1996).

The way to honour the legacy of the Soviet Union is to study it, to learn from its great successes and its sad demise, and to leverage this history towards a global socialist future. Such is the task left to our generation by the Soviet workers. In spite of the rolling back of the first wave of socialist advance, Marxism remains as relevant as ever, and socialism has a bright future in the world.

References

1991. 'Texts of Declarations by 3 Republic Leaders'. *New York Times*, December 9.

1996. 'Fidel Castro In Vietnam'. *Workers World*, January 18.

2010. 'Leader of failed Soviet coup dies'. *Al Jazeera*, September 24.

2015. 'Booze booboo: Gorbachev admits USSR mid-80s anti-alcohol campaign 'too hasty''. *Russia Today*, May 15.

2015. 'Interview with the GDR's Margot Honecker – "The past was brought back"'. *Workers World*, November 16.

2015. 'Kazakhstan: Villagers put Stalin back on pedestal'. *BBC*. May 14.

Amin, Samir. 2014. 'Saving the Unity of Great Britain, Breaking the Unity of Greater Russia'. *Monthly Review*, vol. 66, no. 7, December 1.

Amin, Samir. 2016. *Russia and the Long Transition from Capitalism to Socialism*. New York: Monthly Review Press.

Andropov, Yuri. 1983. *Speeches and Writings*. Oxford and New York: Pergamon Press.

Andropov, Yuri. 1982. *Report on 60th anniversary of the USSR*. December 21.

Aurthur, Jonathan. 1977. *Socialism in the Soviet Union*. Chicago: Workers Press.

Berliner, Jeff. 1991. 'Yeltsin bans Communist Party'. *UPI*, November 6.

Braithwaite, Rodric. 2011. *Afgantsy*. London: Profile Books.

Buckley, Mark. 2017. 'The economic legacy of October 1917'. *Socialist Action*, October 25.

Castro, Fidel, Raúl Castro, and Nelson Mandela. 2013. *Cuba and Angola: Fighting for Africa's Freedom and Our Own*. Atlanta, GA: Pathfinder Press.

Chang, Ha-Joon. 2014. *Economics: A User's Guide*. Pelican.

Chernyaev, Anatoly. 2000. *My Six Years with Gorbachev*. University Park: Pennsylvania State University Press.

Clines, Francis X. 1983. 'Reagan Denounces Ideology of Soviet as "Focus of Evil"'. *New York Times*, March 9.

Cohen, Stephen. 'The breakup of the Soviet Union ended Russia's march to democracy'. *The Guardian*, December 13.

Curtis, Glenn E. (ed.). 1998. *Russia: a country study*. Washington, DC: Federal Research Division, Library of Congress.

Efron, Sonni. 1994. 'Infectious diseases flourishing in former U.S.S.R. as living standards fall'. *Los Angeles Times*, September 20.

Enfu, Cheng, and Liu Zixu. 2017. 'The Historical Contribution of the October Revolution to the Economic and Social Development of the Soviet Union – Analysis of the Soviet Economic Model and the Causes of Its Dramatic End'. *International Critical Thought*, vol. 7, no. 3.

Fein, Esther B. 1991. 'Yeltsin Bans Communist Groups in Government'. *New York Times*, July 21.

Foner, Philip S. 1998. *Paul Robeson Speaks: Writings, Speeches, Interviews, 1918–74*. Kensington Publishing Corp.

Friedman, Jeremy. 2015. *Shadow Cold War: The Sino-Soviet Competition for the Third World*. Chapel Hill, NC: University of North Carolina Press.

Gibbs, David N. 2000. 'Afghanistan: The Soviet Invasion in Retrospect'. *International Politics*, vol. 37, no. 2.

Gorbachev, Mikhail. 2000. *Gorbachev: On My Country and the World*. Columbia University Press.

Gowans, Stephen. 2012. 'Khrushchev's Revisionism'. *Proletarian Center for Research, Education and Culture* (blog), December 29. https://prolecenter.wordpress.com/2012/12/29/khrushchevs-revisionism/.

Habib, Irfan. 2017. 'The Road to the October Revolution in Russia, 1917'. In *Red October: The Russian Revolution and the Communist Horizon*, edited by Vijay Prashad. New Delhi: LeftWord Books.

Halliday, Fred. 1978. 'Revolution in Afghanistan'. *New Left Review*, no. 112.

Hanson, Philip. 2014. *The Rise and Fall of the Soviet Economy: An Economic History of the USSR from 1945*. New York: Routledge.

Johnson, Hewlett. 1939. *The Socialist Sixth of the World*. London: Victor Gollancz.

Keeran, Roger, and Thomas Kenny. 2004. *Socialism Betrayed: Behind the*

Collapse of the Soviet Union. New York: International Publishers.

Keller, Bill. 1988. 'Gorbachev Asks Editors to End Perestroika Debate'. *New York Times*, May 11.

Kendall, Bridget. 2011. 'New light shed on 1991 anti-Gorbachev coup'. *BBC*, August 18.

Kotz, David M. 2017. 'One Hundred Years after the Russian Revolution: Looking Back and Looking Forward'. *International Critical Thought*, vol. 7, no. 3.

Kotz, David M., and Fred Weir. 1997. *Revolution From Above: The Demise of the Soviet System*. Routledge.

Ligachev, Yegor. 1996. *Inside Gorbachev's Kremlin: The Memoirs of Yegor Ligachev*. Boulder, CO, Oxford: Westview Press.

Lin, Justin Yifu. 2011. *Demystifying the Chinese Economy*. Cambridge University Press.

Lynch, Allen. 2012. 'Deng's and Gorbachev's Reform Strategies Compared'. *Russia in Global Affairs*, no. 2, June 24.

Mandel, William. 1985. *Soviet But Not Russian: The 'other' peoples of the Soviet Union*. Palo Alto: Ramparts Press.

Marcy, Sam. 1990. *Perestroika: A Marxist Critique*. New York: WW Publishers.

Motte, Bruni de la, and John Green. 2015. *Stasi State or Socialist Paradise?: The German Democratic Republic and What Became of It*. Artery Publications.

Parenti, Michael. 2001. *Blackshirts and Reds: Rational Fascism and the Overthrow of Communism*. City Lights Publishers.

Ponomarev, Boris. 1983. *Marxism-Leninism in Today's World: A Living and Effective Teaching (A Reply to Critics)*. Oxford and New York: Pergamon Press.

Prashad, Vijay. 2014. *The Poorer Nations: A Possible History of the Global South*. Verso.

Ranadive, B.T. 1987. 'Seventy Glorious Years: Achievements and Problems'. In *Red October: The Russian Revolution and the Communist Horizon*, edited by Vijay Prashad. New Delhi: LeftWord Books.

Roberts, Michael. 2017. 'The Russian revolution: some economic notes'. *Michael Roberts Blog* (blog). https://thenextrecession.wordpress.com/2017/11/08/the-russian-revolution-some-economic-notes/.

Schmemann, Serge. 1988. 'Soviet Union Ends Years of Jamming of Radio Liberty'. *New York Times*, December 1.

Shambaugh, David. 2008. *China's Communist Party: Atrophy and Adaptation*. Berkeley: University of California Press.

Shenming, Li. 2017. 'The October Revolution: A New Epoch in the World History'. *International Critical Thought*, vol. 7, no. 2.

Smith, Evan. 2014. 'Khrushchev Gives "Secret Speech" to 20th Congress of the CPSU'. *Hatful of History* (blog). https://hatfulofhistory.wordpress.com/2014/02/25/feb-25-1956-khrushchev-gives-secret-speech-to-20th-congress-of-the-cpsu/.

Steele, Jonathan. 2003. 'Red Kabul Revisited'. *The Guardian*, November 13.

Szymanski, Albert. 1979. *Is the Red Flag Flying?: The Political Economy of the Soviet Union Today*. London: Zed Press.

Szymanski, Albert. 1984. *Human Rights in the Soviet Union*. London: Zed Books.

Taylor, Adam. 2016. 'Why do so many people miss the Soviet Union?'. *The Washington Post*, December 21.

Westad, Odd Arne. 2005. *The Global Cold War: Third World Interventions and the Making of Our Times*. Cambridge: Cambridge University Press.

Woodward, Jude. 2017. *The US vs China: Asia's new Cold War?*. Manchester: Manchester University Press.

Xiaoping, Deng. 1980. 'Answers to the Italian Journalist Oriana Fallaci'. August 21 and 23.

Yakovlev, Alexander. 1993. *The Fate of Marxism in Russia*. New Haven, CT: Yale University Press.

Yechury, Sitaram. 1991. 'Economy: Reforms for Restoration of Capitalism'. In *Red October: The Russian Revolution and the Communist Horizon*, edited by Vijay Prashad. New Delhi: LeftWord Books.

Zubok, Vladislav. 2009. *A Failed Empire: The Soviet Union in the Cold War from Stalin to Gorbachev*. Chapel Hill, NC: University of North Carolina Press.

Zyuganov, Gennady, and Vadim Medish. 1997. *My Russia: The Political Autobiography of Gennady Zyuganov*. New York: Routledge.